BRITAIN'S FOLKLORE YEAR

Mark Norman

BRITAIN'S FOLKLORE YEAR

National Trust

Published by National Trust Books
An imprint of HarperCollins Publishers
1 London Bridge Street,
London SE1 9GF www.harpercollins.co.uk

HarperCollins Publishers
Macken House, 39/40 Mayor Street Upper,
Dublin 1, D01 C9W8, Ireland

First published 2025
© National Trust Books 2025
Text © Mark Norman 2025
Illustrations © Frank Duffy 2025

ISBN 978-0-00-869796-9
10 9 8 7 6 5 4 3 2 1

The contents of this publication are believed correct at the time of printing. Nevertheless, the publisher can accept no responsibility for errors or omissions, changes in the detail given or for any expense or loss thereby caused.

A catalogue record for this book is available from the British Library.

Printed and bound in India by Replika Press Pvt. Ltd.

If you would like to comment on any aspect of this book, please contact us at the above address or national.trust@harpercollins.co.uk

National Trust publications are available at National Trust shops or online at nationaltrustbooks.co.uk

CONTENTS

Introduction

We interact with folklore every day. Probably many times. It might be something obvious. How often do you avoid walking under a ladder? Or salute a magpie? You might have a lucky object, or a ritual that you perform before a job interview, or other meaningful event. You might have certain family traditions that happen regularly.

Folklore is vital to us as human beings. It allows us to understand who we are, our culture and our place in society. That is because folklore brings with it a sense of identity. It is what makes us part of our community, part of the landscape around us (wherever that landscape may be) and part of a shared understanding of our role in life. If we have

Developments in modern technology have influenced how we view and experience folklore today.

shared interests with others, whether it's knitting, drama, dancing or following a particular band or singer, then we are part of a folk group.

The 19th and early 20th centuries saw a surge of interest in folklore, when the Victorians and Edwardians started collecting material about traditional customs. It was, in part, a response to the increasing urbanisation during the Industrial Revolution. It was an attempt to preserve the past by recording the lives of rural people; what they did and how they did it.

Another wave came after the Second World War, possibly as a reaction to the prevailing global tensions. A sense of nostalgia, and a search for simpler, safer times, had a large part to play.

In the 21st century, similar anxieties have fed into another folklore revival, while also taking on new meanings. Developments in modern technology have influenced how we view and experience folklore today, with a growing field of 'digital folklore' allowing us to form links with the global folklore community and other cultures.

Our existing customs and traditions are not necessarily subsumed by these new developments – indeed, they can be enhanced by them. For example, English Heritage livestream the sunrise over Stonehenge in Wiltshire at the summer solstice, allowing people from around the world to witness this magical spectacle and become a part of the rituals performed there.

A note on dates

The annual events that make up the folklore year in Britain can be divided into two distinct categories: **fixed** and **moveable**.

The distinction is fairly obvious. Fixed events occur on the same calendar date each year, such as St George's Day (23 April) or Oak Apple Day (29 May). Moveable dates might relate to customs being tied to certain days of the month, such as the Ceres Highland Games on the last Saturday of June. Festivals within the liturgical or Christian church calendar are sometimes more complicated. For example, Easter is determined by the timing of the spring equinox and the lunar cycle (which certainly sounds more scientific than religious).

Some of these complications arose in 1582 when Pope Gregory XIII replaced the existing Julian calendar and ten days were 'lost'. His new Gregorian calendar was adopted by Britain in 1752, changing the dates of fixed calendrical festivals and customs. Christmas Day became 25 December, with 6 January becoming known as Old Christmas. We can see this today in terms of how we celebrate these days, with 25 December focusing on the birth of Christ, while older practices such as wassailing and house-visiting traditions taking place on 6 January.

The meteorological and astronomical year

In another quirk of folklore, there are also two ways of defining the seasonal year: the astronomical year and the meteorological year. **Astronomical** seasons refer to the position of Earth's orbit in relation to the sun, with each season defined by the equinoxes and solstices, the dates of which vary by a day or so, year on year. **Meteorological** seasons split the year into four fixed periods of three months based on the annual temperature cycles to allow us to record and compare statistics.

Many traditions featured in this book follow the astronomical seasons. However, as these do not coincide with the meteorological seasons, for certainty and completeness the dates for both are given at the start of each chapter.

Calendar cycles and the Wheel of the Year

Lying at the heart of our ritual year is the cycle of the seasons. While agriculture and food production are still an important part of the economy, in times gone by these were vital to the survival of communities. The cycle of preparation, planting, nurturing and harvesting relates strongly to both celebration and superstition. The themes of death and rebirth, fertility and growth can be found in many of our customs to this day.

In terms of festivals, the yearly cycle is made up of eight celebrations. The four main ones are the vernal (or spring) and autumn equinoxes, and the summer and winter solstices – the word solstice coming from the Latin *sol* ('sun') and *sistere* ('to stand still'). Between these lie four quarter days. These were historically set aside for legal resolutions, rent collection and the hiring of staff, and fell on Lady Day (the end of March), Midsummer (the end of June), Michaelmas (the end of September) and Christmas (the end of December), and the folklore calendar year is derived from these.

The **Wheel of the Year** is used in relation to the annual cycle of these festivals, often represented artistically as an actual wheel. The initial idea was introduced by the German folklorist, and co-author of the famous Grimms' fairytales, Jacob Grimm in his 1835 book *Teutonic Mythology*. The eight festivals we now associate with the Wheel of the Year were then fixed by prominent figures in the traditions of Wicca and Druidry (both of which draw on Celtic paganism) from the mid-1950s.

These days, the most common names used for these eight celebrations are:

* **Samhain**   (31 October)
* **Yule**   (20–25 December)
* **Imbolc**   (1–2 February)
* **Ostara**   (20–23 March)
* **Beltane**   (30 April–1 May)
* **Litha**   (20–22 June)
* **Lughnasadh**   (1 August)
* **Mabon**   (20–23 September)

For each season, *Britain's Folklore Year* features a selection of well-known and more obscure customs and traditions – from those of the ancient Celts, travelling through the centuries, changing and adapting, to others that have been revived or have emerged in modern times. Together they paint a picture of the ritual year and give a flavour of the culturally diverse range of celebrations and festivities, both national and local, that comprise it. From hobby horse ceremonies in the south-west of England to the Ba' game in Scotland's Orkney Isles, from the Gŵyl Awst festival in Wales to the making of Brigid's Crosses in Ireland, the following pages will explore all that makes the British Isles so special.

And don't worry. No wicker men. Well, not many anyway ...

Meteorological spring:
1 March to 31 May

Astronomical spring:
Vernal equinox (near 20 March)
to summer solstice (near 21 June)

Frost-locked all the winter,
Seeds, and roots, and stones of fruits,
What shall make their sap ascend
That they may put forth shoots?
Tips of tender green,
Leaf, or blade, or sheath;
Telling of the hidden life
That breaks forth underneath,
Life nursed in its grave by Death.

'Spring' by Christina Rossetti (1830–94)

Spring

Springtime has a number of customs with a great variety of rituals. Although we find saints' days in the calendar all through the year, some of the big names come up in the spring, with St George for England, St David for Wales and St Patrick for Ireland all being celebrated at this time. Over the years, England has somewhat neglected its celebrations, although there has been a recent attempt to redress this in London with St George's Day festivities happening in Trafalgar Square. Both Wales and Ireland, however, proudly play host to many events for their patron saints.

Easter might be the celebration that most quickly springs to mind but there are other springtime celebrations of a slightly different flavour, full of historic interest, such as Mother's Day and April Fools' Day. And let us not forget more local events, such as the Helston Flora Day in Cornwall, Cheese Rolling in Gloucestershire and Hallaton Bottle Kicking in Leicestershire.

If we consider the cycle of the seasons, it is easy to see how spring would have been an important time for our ancestors. Emerging from a long, cold and harsh winter that would have inevitably depleted food supplies, the first signs of life starting to appear would have felt like a blessing from the gods. With the shoots of recovery and the first glimpses of green came the chance to begin to plant the seeds that would hopefully yield a good harvest later in the year. As such, many of the festivals and celebrations at this time have strong connections with life and fertility.

Vernal Equinox and Ostara

The beginning of spring in the old calendar was marked by the vernal (or spring) equinox, which some pagans today call **Ostara**. This is a time when day and night are of equal length, and are thus considered to be in balance, with masculine and feminine energies also being in tune. Rebirth and growth are important themes and, like Easter, symbols include eggs and rabbits. We might think of the egg in terms of fertility, but it also resembles the balance which comes with the equal length of days and nights. The female goddess and male god are reflected in the white and yolk of the egg – the yellow yolk represents the sun god while the white represents the purity of the goddess. Symbolically, the dead land presided over by the Holly King in winter is now taken back by summer's Oak King, allowing life to flourish once more.

The term Ostara is derived from the Germanic goddess of spring, Ēostre. Much discussion is devoted to what connections there may be between this goddess, and this spring festival, with the Christian celebration of Easter. One of the most popular memes to be found on the internet around this subject claims that the word 'Easter' comes from the Babylonian fertility goddess, Ishtar. However, this assertion, originally made in the 19th century in an anti-Catholic pamphlet, should be treated with a certain degree of scepticism.

Lent

Lent – the six-week period of fasting and charity that comes before Easter, the most important time in the Christian year – has fewer traditions than the main event. However, there are still places that observe customs relating to Shrove Tuesday, the day before the beginning of Lent.

Shrove Tuesday

Shrove Tuesday was traditionally a time to use up eggs and fat before fasting began. Making pancakes was a popular way to do this, which is why Shrove Tuesday is often known as Pancake Day. At the start of the Lent period it was necessary to attend church to be 'shriven' (absolved from sins) and the church rang a shriving bell for this event. It is said that the popular pancake race tradition we know today goes back to the 15th century, when a woman was said to have dashed to church while running late, still holding her frying pan – complete with pancake. But there are other traditions too.

In the Dorset village of Durweston, the local primary school children still observe a house-visiting tradition. They will hand over small posies of flowers to those answering the door and sing a **shroving song**, and in return hope for a small donation of money from the householder. Nowadays, this money is used to purchase resources for the school.

A similar custom is observed at East Hendred in Oxfordshire but here the children visit the manor house instead. Again, they sing a shroving song and each child receives a penny and a fruit bun.

Easter

Easter is an established part of our secular calendar, marking Jesus's crucifixion and resurrection. The lead up to Easter Sunday sees the solemnity of Holy Week (also known as Passion Week), which includes Palm Sunday, Maundy Thursday and Good

Friday, culminating in the joyous (and tasty) customs and celebrations of Easter Day.

Many of the symbols that we associate with Easter are difficult to pin down. Across the north of Europe there is a strong connection with **hares and rabbits**, because of their associations with fertility and new life at this time. From this comes the concept of the Easter Bunny, hopping merrily through the countryside, liberally dishing out chocolate eggs and other treats to all and sundry.

Eggs and egg customs

Eggs were seen to symbolise rebirth in Christianity from as early as the 1st century AD, but possibly their strongest association with Easter came in the Middle Ages when they were banned during Lent, along with other meat and animal products. In England, house-visiting traditions used to take place on the Saturday before fasting began, with children asking for real eggs as a treat. Now, whether we abstain from eating treats during Lent or not, many of us look forward to eggs of the chocolate kind when Easter finally arrives!

Celebrations still take place in Preston, Lancashire, at Avenham and Miller Parks, where many children enjoy **traditional egg-rolling**. The winner is the person whose egg rolls the furthest distance down one of the grass hills without cracking. While it was said to be good luck for your egg to stay intact, at the end of the event any bits of shell left behind on the slopes would be destroyed by the children. This comes from

a much older belief found all around the country: that local witches would otherwise use the shells as boats to sail out to sea and sink fishing boats.

A relatively well-known Easter custom from the north of England connected with this theme is the **Pace Egg play**. The term 'pace' here may derive from the Latin *pasche*, or 'passion', explaining its association with Easter time.

The play is not unlike the traditional mummers' plays performed by masked amateur actors during winter festivals. Both follow in the same tradition of medieval mystery plays recounting biblical tales through tableau and song. Pace Egg plays take place on Good Friday. The story tells of a mock combat between the hero (sometimes St George) and a villain. The hero will be slain during the play, only to be brought back to life by a quack doctor or similar comical figure. The theme of spring rebirth is central here.

Among the other characters in the troupe is the traditional Fool. Their role is usually to taunt the audience, clown around and often to help solicit donations from onlookers. In the Pace Egg play, this character is called Old Tosspot, a name still used in slang to this day to denote someone foolish and annoying.

Pace Eggers, as the actors were known, would travel from village to village performing their play. They would sometimes receive decorated Pace Eggs as gifts for this – part of a worldwide tradition of painting eggs at Easter.

If you'd like to make your own Pace Eggs, the usual method is to hard boil the eggs while they are wrapped in onion skin, flowers or leaves. This creates a mottled shell that can then be further decorated.

Although Pace Egging is not as common now as it used to be, records show that it used to be very popular. The household accounts of King Edward I for the year 1290, for example, include an entry for 'one shilling and sixpence for the decoration and distribution of 450 Pace-eggs'.

Easter competitions and events

As well as the many recognisable events that take place over Easter weekend, there are also plenty of obscure ones. If you don't want to go Pace Egging on Good Friday, then you might like to participate in the **British Marble Championships**, which also reaches its climax on this date. These are held at the

Greyhound Pub in Tinsley Green, West Sussex, and date back in their current form to 1932, although there is a marble-playing tradition here that goes back many centuries. One tradition holds that this comes from a game played in 1588 by two young local men to decide which one should be able to marry a woman they both liked.

Players travel from all over the world to take part in the championships. A variant of the game, called Ring Taw, uses 49 target marbles within a concrete ring, 6 foot in diameter and covered in sand. A complicated set of rules governs how the shooting marble (the tolley) is fired into the circle. The first team to remove 25 marbles from the circle are the winners.

If marbles are too small to satisfy your competitive needs, then you could always wait a couple of days until Easter Monday, and pop over to the northern English village of Gawthorpe in West Yorkshire, and try your luck in the **World Coal Carrying Championships**.

Different races take place for different categories, with the men's, women's and veterans' being the main three. Competitors must run a 1,000-metre course carrying a sack of coal on their backs – 50 kilogrammes for men and 20 kilogrammes for women. Times are recorded using both stopwatches and an original pigeon-racing clock. Anyone breaking the record time for the course wins a cash prize.

Becoming so popular that three men's races have to be run instead of the original one, the World Coal Carrying Championships have been going since 1963. It is thought that the race came about as the result of a wager in a local pub between two men as to who could carry a sack of coal between the bar and the village green the fastest. Stories vary, however, as to who the two men were. Some say it was a farmer and coal merchant; others that it was a farmer and a miner. Either, of course, have a coal connection.

In terms of folklore, many stories come about because of a wager, although often they centre around the ghost of a person who died because of the bet. Thankfully, in this case, everyone is very much alive.

If you want to witness a much rougher and more furious competition, then the Leicestershire village of Hallaton is the place to be. Every Easter Monday, the **Hallaton Bottle Kicking** contest pits villagers against those from nearby Medbourne, with the aim of taking control of a keg of beer, or more precisely three kegs.

The aim is to be the first team to move two of the three kegs over the stream and into your home village. This usually takes somewhere around five hours to complete, with something like an estimated 7,000 people taking part across the two opposing sides.

The Bottle Kicking competition, and its accompanying event the **Hare Pie Scramble**, are very old customs, said to be pre-Christian in origin and are certainly more than two centuries old. Before the Bottle Kicking takes place, a large hare pie is paraded to the church gates, and then on to an area nearby where it is broken up, or 'scrambled', and thrown into the crowd. Local tradition has it that two women from Hallaton were once crossing a field when a bull spotted them and charged. They were saved by a hare in the field, which distracted the bull and allowed them to escape.

As a gesture of thanks, they made a gift of land to the Church, with an accompanying covenant stating that a hare pie, loaves and barrels of ale must be given by the Church to the poor every Easter Monday. When the residents of the neighbouring village arrived and fought the Hallaton folk for their food and drink one year, the competition was born.

One of the more obscure and curious customs that took place at this time of the year was **Easter Lifting**.

Hare pie, loaves and barrels of ale were given by the Church to the poor every Easter Monday.

This was exactly what the name implies: two or more people lifting another high into the air. In some cases, this might take the form of two people joining crossed hands in the fashion of a makeshift chair. In others, it would be a group of people lifting (or 'heaving', the alternative name for the practice) someone sitting on an actual chair.

Lifting traditionally took place on Easter Monday and Tuesday. On the former, the men would lift the women and, on the latter, the other way around ... providing the women could catch the men of course. As with many customs, a demand for a small cash offering would often be made, although sometimes this was replaced with a request for a kiss.

Interestingly, there were no inhibitions about rank or class with this custom. The local squire or parson was fair game to be lifted if they were caught. One report tells of a squire paying five shillings to avoid a lifting. Another, quoted in Robert Chamber's *The Book of Days* (1864), has a clergyman in a Lancashire town paying half a crown to a group of women at an inn he was staying in to 'escape the dreaded compliment'.

As far as the origin of this custom is concerned, we cannot say for certain. Some believe that it's linked to some kind of fertility rite, but this may just be because it takes place in the spring. Another school of thought is that it's a parody or re-enactment of Christ's resurrection – we can never know for sure.

There seems to be only one modern revival of this tradition in Britain now. Blackheath Morris Team, in Greenwich, London, carry out Easter Lifting as part of their first outing of the season.

Lifting of a different kind happens at Dorking in Surrey each March at the annual **Wife Carrying Race**. While this is a newer tradition, it does have an older origin that can apparently be traced to Scandinavia: legend says that the race grew out of tests of fitness by Viking raiders who would steal women from other villages in their area.

A detailed explanation of the event is probably not required: pick up your wife, holding her legs over your shoulders so she is pointing head-first down your back, and then run the 380-metre course quicker than anyone else.

The rules are pretty lax – you don't have to be married to your 'wife' to take part and the wife can be of any gender. However, the 'wife' *does* have to wear a safety helmet. The prizes are about as impressive as the rules: beer for the winners and novelty prizes (such as Pot Noodle or dog food) for the runners-up.

Charitable gifts

Customs linked to this time of year include the distribution of doles to the poor. One ancient example dating back to the 13th century is the **Tichborne Dole**, handed out each **Lady Day**, 25 March, in the form of flour milled from wheat grown on The Crawls, near Alresford in Hampshire. The story goes that Lady Mabella Tichborne, mortally ill, asked her miserly husband to make an annual donation of food to the poor of the parish. He agreed on one condition: that she crawl around a field holding a flaming torch before it went out. Despite being close to death, she did so.

The story has become famous, along with the curse which she allegedly placed on her husband and any of his heirs if they stopped the dole being distributed.

Another story, of disputed origin, is found at Biddenden in Kent. Every Easter Monday, hard biscuits

When Mary died, Eliza refused to allow doctors to try and separate them.

known as Biddenden cakes are distributed, an ancient practice known as the **Biddenden Dole**. The legend relates to conjoined twins, Mary and Eliza Chulkhurst, who were born here in 1100 and are now represented on the village sign. When Mary died, Eliza refused to allow doctors to try and separate them, passing away six hours later. In their will, the Biddenden Maids, as they became known, left five pieces of land to the church; the

income from this land was to be given to the poor in the form of bread and cheese each Easter.

Biddenden cakes bear an image of the two women, along with their names and the numbers 34 (their age when they died) and 1100 (their year of birth), commemorating the story of their charitable donation.

But rarely is everything in folklore as clear-cut as it appears. Some documentary evidence from the 18th century suggests that the lands donated to the church came from two women named Preston, or alternatively that the gift was made anonymously.

Hocktide

The Monday and Tuesday of the second week after Easter is known as Hocktide. The term is not heard much nowadays, but this was a significant medieval festival. Aside from Whitsun (see page 38) and the Christmas period, the week after Easter was the only time a holiday was granted to those who worked on the land, marking the start of the busy planting season.

The Tuesday of Hocktide was also one of the days on which rents were payable. It fell, like Michaelmas, on 29 September, a formal date for splitting the year into summer and winter. In order to raise funds for the church, women would capture local men at this time, tying them up and demanding a fee for their release.

> *Easter was the only time a holiday was granted to those who worked on the land, marking the start of the busy planting season.*

Hocktide celebrations can still be found at Hungerford in Berkshire, where the **Hocktide Court** is held on the second Tuesday after Easter, also known as **Tutti Day**. In the 14th century, Hungerford was granted hunting and fishing rights by John of Gaunt and it is this that the modern festival remembers.

Although the celebrations cover a longer period, Tutti Day and the traditional lunch in Hungerford's Town Hall are considered the highlight. The day itself is acted out in memory of the original rent collecting, or gathering of tithes, which is associated with Hock Tuesday. This ritual collection is undertaken by **Tithing Men**, known here as **Tutti Men** despite the fact that both men and women take the roles.

Commoners (those who live in the area and are thus still able to exercise the rights granted by John of Gaunt) are summoned to the Town Hall by the blowing of a horn by the **Bellman**. The horn belongs to the **Constable**, who hands out Tithing Poles, decorated with flowers and topped with an orange, to the Tutti Men.

The orange might seem a curious detail, but there is an explanation: in the 17th century, Hungerford supported William of Orange's claim to the throne of England and this is what is being recalled. Now, rather than collecting money, the tithes gathered are kisses, and an orange is given in return.

After a formal lunch takes place, there is another custom known as the **Shoeing of the Colts**. The 'colts' are newcomers who have not attended the lunch before. They are grabbed by the blacksmith who pretends to hammer a nail into their shoe. This continues until the colt shouts 'punch'. A little struggling is encouraged so as not to make the shoeing too easy for the smith, although ladies are often shod sitting down for their own comfort, if they so choose.

At the end of the afternoon there is a traditional serving of anchovies on toast and a performance by the town band before the Tutti Men return to the Town Hall, well into the evening, presumably having distributed a lot of oranges.

May Day and Beltane

In the UK there are two bank holidays in May, one at the beginning of the month and the other at the end. The first of these celebrates May Day, a key date in the British folk calendar. The medieval tradition of feasting and dancing to mark the day has its roots in three other ancient festivals – the fires of Beltane, Walpurgisnacht (the feast day of St Walpurgis) and Floralia (the Roman festival celebrating the goddess Flora). Festivities to mark the event were banned by the Puritans in the 1640s, but King Charles II, lover of many a good party, reinstated May Day as a celebration after his restoration to the throne 20 years later.

One of those original festivals, and still very much observed today, is the Celtic festival of **Beltane**, literally 'fires of Bel' – the second of the calendar year's quarter day festivals.

A large fire festival providing a reinterpretation of the original Beltane celebrations takes place every year at Calton Hill in Edinburgh, a location topped by many monuments. A procession begins from the top of the hill, accompanied by drums, and makes its way downhill in an anti-clockwise direction. As the parade makes its way – led by two common characters of spring folklore, the **May Queen** and the **Green Man** – the group is met by a number of other characters, who will either aid them or obstruct their progress. The procession ends with a stage performance symbolising the coming of summer, and the lighting of a huge bonfire.

The name of the **Celtic god Bel**, associated with the Beltane celebrations, means 'bright one', and bonfires would be lit to honour the sun. Being connected with the needs of the land, Beltane marks the start of the old farming calendar (before the advent of modern farming methods). This is why fertility is so closely linked to spring, and why the old nature-based religions considered that the energy of the earth and sexual potency peaked now.

In the Calton Hill celebration, the procession of the May Queen and the Green Man represents new life and rebirth. This symbolic union is the reason why pagan wedding ceremonies, known as **handfastings**, are very popular around May Day.

Decoration was important on May Day, and people would collect flowers, greenery and tree blossom to adorn their homes, singing as they did so. The popular children's playground rhyme 'Here we go gathering nuts in May' probably derives from this. As it is written now, the rhyme makes little sense as nuts are green this early in the year and no good for eating. Perhaps the original version of the rhyme went 'Here we go gathering knots of May,' which refers to the sprays of May (hawthorn) blossom.

Maypoles

Maypoles and **maypole dancing** is a quintessential part of May Day festivities. Participants in this celebration of the coming season dance around the pole holding coloured ribbons that are woven into intricate patterns. At one time such dances would take place in almost every school in England.

The maypole was a place on which to hang greenery and other garlands as decoration, which were an important part of May Day traditions. The foliage-bedecked pole was originally the focal point for circle dances. The ribbons we all associate with the maypole are a much later addition, with the earliest example appearing in the 1830s. The Victorians and Edwardians popularised the use of ribbons as part of the view of 'Merrie England', and thus we automatically think of maypoles today in this form.

In terms of public performances, there are now around 70 permanent maypoles in Britain. One of these can be found in the village of Wellow, Nottinghamshire, in the heart of

Robin Hood's own Sherwood Forest. While the legendary outlaw may be something of an invention, this maypole most certainly is not, and is considered unique for having an angular 18-sided (octadecagon) pole.

There has been a maypole at Wellow since the middle of the 19th century; the current one was installed in 2011 to replace its predecessor, which had become corroded. Each late Spring Bank Holiday, a new May Queen is crowned and dancing displays take place alongside other live entertainment and a fête.

The early origins of the maypole are uncertain. The first written references come from the 14th century, with the earliest representation probably from a Tudor-era window in Staffordshire.

As you might expect, there are suggestions of links between the phallic maypole rising from the earth and spring fertility rituals, but there is no definite evidence for this connection. What we can say is that maypole dancing is, and always has been, an event which brings communities together.

Hobby horses

A stalwart of many of the early spring bank holiday customs is the hobby horse. This can take many different forms, depending on the area of the country in which it takes place. Arguably the most well-known example can be found in the Cornish fishing port of Padstow. For centuries, every **May Day**, two hobby

horses have been led through the streets, and the event can draw many thousands of spectators.

Here the creatures are known as **'obby 'osses**, with the dropped 'h' being reminiscent of the Cornish accent. Before the First World War there was just a single hobby horse, known as the **old 'oss**. Jet black in colour, it takes the form of a large hoop, worn on the shoulders by the carrier, whose head sticks out of the top and is covered by a conical mask. There are definite associations with spring fertility with this 'oss, which traditionally tries to capture young women under its skirt. To be captured by the 'oss meant that you could expect to fall pregnant soon afterwards.

In 1919, a second 'oss was added to the ceremony. This is known as the **blue ribbon 'oss** but is also called the **temperance 'oss**. The name harks back to its original introduction by those who were making a stand against the drunken behaviour that was associated with this festival. A friendly rivalry exists between the two 'osses, which are accompanied by a teaser (who leads them), and a procession of musicians and dancers.

The hooped design of the hobby horse at Padstow seems to be unique to the south-west of England, and two similar ceremonies still take place in the region. The first of these, which is held around May Day, is in the Somerset town of Minehead.

The **Original Sailors Horse** was accompanied only by a drum, whereas the **Traditional Sailors Horse** is now serenaded by drummers and musicians; there is also the **Town Horse**. All comprise a sackcloth skirt, painted with coloured circles, and a

WASHING IN THE MAY DEW

The May Day dew was believed to have magical properties. Washing your face with the morning dew on 1 May was thought to mean that your skin would be without blemish for the whole of the following year.

In Edinburgh, thousands of people would climb the extinct volcano known as Arthur's Seat for this purpose and still do so to this day. In 1773, Robert Fergusson wrote about the practice in his poem 'Auld Reikie'.

However, other dates in the month should be avoided. One saying goes: 'Those who bathe in May will soon be laid in clay.'

Laundry was also avoided at this time, by those who superstitiously followed another proverb: 'Wash a blanket in May, you will wash one of the family away.'

frame covered in coloured ribbons. The Minehead horses are boat-shaped rather than being circular.

The third of the hobby horse ceremonies in the South West is perhaps more storied than the other two, and its horse is an amalgamation of the Minehead and Padstow versions. The **Hunting of the Earl of Rone** takes place over the Whitsun weekend in the coastal north Devon village of Combe Martin over a period of four days.

Revived in the 1970s, this custom is based on written descriptions of the original; this used to take place on Ascension Day and was banned in 1837 because of 'drunken and licentious behaviour' – perhaps they needed a temperance 'oss too!

The Earl in this ceremony is Hugh O'Neill, Earl of Tyrone, who fled Ulster in 1607 along with Rory O'Donnell, 1st Earl of Tyrconnell, and around 90 followers. Their exile symbolised the end of the old Gaelic order in Ireland. The ceremony in Combe Martin is based on the story of a party of grenadier soldiers from the nearby town of Barnstaple being sent out to capture the Earl, who had been shipwrecked on the coast and was concealed in woods near the village.

On the Friday evening, the procession is made up of drummers, grenadiers, the hobby horse and Fool (the leader of the horse in this case). Over the weekend, they are joined by musicians and walkers. On the Monday evening, the culmination of the festival, the Earl – played by a child who is masked and dressed in sackcloth – is captured in the woods. The 'Earl' sits back-to-front on a donkey and is paraded down the village to the beach. The party stops many times along the way.

At each stopping point, the Earl is ritually 'shot' by the grenadiers, and then revived by the hobby horse and Fool, before being reseated on the donkey to continue the journey. Here, once again, we can see the ideas of resurrection and rebirth found across many spring customs and traditions.

> *We might think of this as a form of 'sacrifice', made ritually to ensure a good harvest.*

Finally, on reaching the beach, the Earl is shot for the final time. At this point, the real life 'Earl' is switched for an effigy, which is then thrown into the sea by the grenadiers. We might think of this as a form of 'sacrifice', made ritually to ensure a good harvest or a prosperous year ahead.

As far as history goes, the Hunting of the Earl of Rone is on rather shaky ground: Hugh O'Neill was not shipwrecked on the British coast but rather made it safely to the Continent. But folklore never lets the truth get in the way of a good celebration.

Another hobby horse custom, this time found in Kent, is known as **Hoodening** and features a horse of a different design. Here, the head of the horse is mounted on a pole, with sackcloth once again concealing the carrier. This ceremony would sometimes take place at the Spring Bank Holiday, but is more closely associated with Christmas time, so we will meet this horse again later in the year (see page 160).

Whitsun

The second bank holiday in May falls at the end of the month and has since the 1970s been known as the Spring Bank Holiday. Until then, and very much connected with the Christian church, it was known as Whitsun, a name which is still common today.

Whitsun is another name for the religious festival of **Pentecost**, and views on the origin of the word are divided. Some believe that the name comes from the Anglo-Saxon word *wit*, meaning 'understanding', and that this refers to a period of being filled with the knowledge of the Holy Spirit. If this were the case, then the term would have come into use during the first few hundred years after the birth of Christ.

More likely is the suggestion that the name is derived from a contraction of **'White Sunday'**, probably because people baptised on this day would wear white garments. Some folklore seems to bear this out, as it is recorded that girls would attend church wearing white and carrying garlands of white flowers.

> *The name is most likely derived from a contraction of 'White Sunday', probably because people baptised on this day would wear white garments.*

In some areas, Whitsun weekend is the time set for **Beating the Bounds**. This is a custom that still takes place in many parishes around the country. In the past, the parish where you lived was generally the community you belonged to for your whole life: you would be born, get married and die there. Knowing the boundaries of your parish was important for setting tithes, marking areas of responsibility and confirming your identity within the community.

Village boundaries would be marked out with boundary posts. A group of people from the parish would walk the boundary, stopping at each post and beating it in order to 'hammer it' into the minds of the young people. In some parishes, as a more memorable (and certainly more painful) reminder, the young boys would themselves be beaten rather than the marker. In the Dartmoor parish of Belstone in Devon, the oldest member of the parish would hold the youngest boy upside down and bounce him head first onto the boundary stone – thankfully, this tradition no longer takes place!

Many boundary stones in the country were restored as part of the Millennium celebrations, and that has seen an upsurge in the revival of Beating the Bounds. You will undoubtedly be able to find one such event close to where you live. If the ceremony does not happen around Whitsun, then it will be on Ascension Day (or the evening before), as this was another traditional time for the ritual to take place.

A more formal Beating the Bounds happens every year at the Tower of London, with all of the regalia that you would expect on display. The area of London surrounding the Tower is called Tower Liberties, and is independent of the authority of the rest of the City of London. It would have been vital, therefore, that those who lived within the Liberties knew where the boundary lay.

Twenty-two markers survive at the Tower of London and they are beaten every three years in accordance with the original custom. A mock battle can still take place between the two parishes on either side of the boundary (outside the Tower this is the parish of All Hallows), commemorating an actual riot between rival residents in 1698.

Apples and nuts would be thrown into bogs along the route.

The ceremony is usually accompanied by light refreshments, which often form an integral part of folk traditions. The Beating the Bounds in the Devon parish of Bridestowe was so renowned for its wagon loaded with baked goods, that it became known as **Beating the Buns**. In Okehampton in West Devon, where the custom was known as **Spurling Day**, apples and nuts would be thrown into bogs or mires along the route, causing young boys in attendance to scramble for them.

Garlands, flowers and decorations

As we saw in the Introduction (see page 6), the change in the calendar in 1582 impacted the dates of fixed celebrations. In the Dorset village of Abbotsbury, their May Day celebration of **Abbotsbury Garland Day** takes place on 13 May, which is also known as **Old May Day**.

Garland Day celebrations grew out of a custom associated with the fishing fleet. Flower garlands were made by the children of fishing families and then taken to the local church where they were blessed. These were hung on the boats as they went out to sea. As May marked the start of the fishing season, this ceremony once again constitutes a ritual blessing to try and ensure a bountiful catch, in the same way as those relating to planting of crops for a fruitful harvest.

When the local fishing trade began to decline, the ceremony changed and, after the First World War, garlands were paraded on poles before being laid at the war memorial.

At one time or another, many primary school children used to participate in garland making, and this also intersects with the custom of **May dolling**, which was a bit like the 'penny for the guy' tradition associated with 5 November (see page 89). Dolls would be dressed in fine clothes, decorated with greenery and flowers then placed in a box. On receipt of a coin from a generous passer-by or householder, the doll would be revealed.

A very flamboyant garland can be seen at the annual Castleton Garland Day in Derbyshire, which takes place on 29 May.

A very flamboyant garland can be seen at the annual **Castleton Garland Day** in Derbyshire, which takes place on 29 May (or the closest Saturday if it falls on a Sunday). Castleton's garland is large and bell-shaped and is worn by the Garland King, who is paraded on horseback through the village before arriving at the church gates. Here the garland, which weighs some 25 kilogrammes, is removed and hung from the church tower for the next few days.

Over the years, the Castleton ceremony's obscure origins have allowed people's imagination to run wild, with one folklorist in the 1960s suggesting that the event had started life as a ritual that culminated in human sacrifice. While the elaborate garland may evoke images of psychological thriller film *Midsommar*, evidence shows that the custom began in the late 18th to early 19th century, having evolved from the local rushbearing – the old ecclesiastical festival where rushes would be gathered and scattered on the church floor (see page 70).

Castleton's bell-shaped garland is worn by the Garland King.

Well dressing

May sees the start of the custom of **Well Dressing**, with decorations tending to be created throughout the summer until September. Particularly associated with Derbyshire and the Peak District, although also found in a handful of other locations, this is the practice of decorating holy wells with beautiful, themed works of art using flower petals, seeds and other natural materials.

Designs might celebrate particular local connections or events, or something else of historic significance. Teams of people work for days pressing leaves, petals and other items into large beds of clay. Once completed, the floral decorations will be blessed before being placed around the well; they will usually look good for up to a week.

Well Dressing is believed to derive from Roman or Celtic ceremonies of venerating wells to give thanks for the fresh water that they provide. Information is usually given in advance as to where and when modern dressings are happening, making them easy to find and visit.

Sanding the streets

Another unusual artistic custom takes place around May Day at Knutsford in Cheshire. Known as **Sanding the Streets**, this is where mottoes, slogans and other patterns are traced onto paths and pavements using coloured sand. The skills required for sanding were traditionally passed down from one generation to another of a local family.

Although now connected with May Day festivities, sanding used to be a wedding custom in Knutsford. Oral tradition has it that King Canute forded the river here in the 11th century on his way to battle the King of Scotland. While sitting down to shake the sand from his shoes after crossing the river, a bridal party passed by, and Canute wished them a happy life together. And the tradition, allegedly, was born.

If you're going to view the sanding, then hope for good weather as the designs do not fare well in the rain!

Oak Apple Day

The Castleton celebrations (see page 41) share a date with **Oak Apple Day**, which commemorates the restoration of King Charles II to the throne in the 17th century. The name derives from the story of how the future monarch evaded capture by hiding himself in an oak tree.

It was on this date, 29 May 1660, that an Act of Parliament was passed that made Oak Apple Day an official celebration to be held each year. Supporters would wear a sprig of oak to demonstrate that they were loyal to the new king. While the public holiday ceased in 1859, we still see vestiges of Oak Apple Day being celebrated today.

On Oak Apple Day, a new bough is carried to the church and hauled up to the top of the tower on a rope.

In many places, processions are held through the streets, which culminate with the hanging of an oak bough from the church tower, in much the same manner as the garland at Castleton. In the Cornish village of St Neots, the bough remains on the top of the tower all year. On Oak Apple Day, a new bough is carried to the church and hauled up to the top of the tower on a rope. The old bough is tossed down and the festivities end with a barbecue on the vicarage lawn.

A ceremony at Great Wishford in Wiltshire dates back to 1603, when a royal charter granted villagers the right to collect firewood from Grovely Wood all through the year, as well as foraging and pasturing cattle there. The day begins with a form of 'rough music' as people process through the street banging pots and pans and ringing bells to wake the villagers. Once everyone is gathered, they head to the woods to collect oak boughs to decorate their houses and the church tower as at St Neots.

The villagers then march from Great Wishford to Salisbury Cathedral, led by women bearing oak branches. A banner is carried which proclaims, 'Grovely! Grovely! Grovely! And All Grovely! Unity is Strength', and a similar proclamation is made at the cathedral altar. Afterwards, expect food and drink and a maypole dance back at Great Wishford.

Flora Day

Keen to extend the May Day celebrations, on 8 May (or on the Saturday before if that date falls on a Sunday or a Monday) the Cornish village of Helston holds **Helston Flora Day**, which attracts thousands of visitors. Here they can watch many hundreds of couples, both adults and children, dressed in their finest clothes dancing through the streets in grand formation. The procession takes a route that has been used for many years, even passing through shops and houses.

The dance performed is known as the **Furry Dance**, with its name possibly deriving from the Cornish word *fer*, which means 'fair' or 'feast'. Traditionally, the villagers would first head into the woods or fields to gather flowers and foliage with which to

THE DUMB CAKE

Dumb cakes were baked on St Mark's Eve
(24 April) by young women who wished to divine
who their future husband would be. Baked in silence
(hence the name), the cakes would include the
following ingredients:

An eggshell full of salt

An eggshell full of wheatmeal

An eggshell full of barleymeal

They were baked in a fire just before
midnight, by a solitary woman who had been fasting.
She then cut the cake into three, eating one part and
placing the rest under her pillow. As midnight tolled,
the woman walked backwards up the stairs and got
quietly into bed. If she was going to be married, then
the dumb cake would allow her to dream
of her future husband.

decorate their houses and themselves. Today, the town is wonderfully decorated with greenery, including bluebells and hazel. This is, naturally, a celebration of the first signs of spring, echoing the themes of so many of the customs taking place around this time.

If you want to see the main dance, then it begins on the stroke of noon, although there are others in the early morning and at 5pm. The music will be instantly recognisable to those over a certain age, having been popularised by Terry Wogan's version of the 'Floral Dance', released in 1978. The original song was written in 1911 by Katie Moss after a visit to the town. The traditional version of the music, played only by the Helston Town Band for the event, has no written score but is passed down from one band leader to the next.

There is an alternative legend, which suggests that Flora Day commemorates the occasion when a dragon dropped a large rock onto the town.

Although undoubtedly deriving from early springtime rituals and celebrations, there is also an alternative legend. This suggests that Flora Day commemorates the occasion when a passing dragon dropped a large rock onto the town. Fortunately the Helston residents survived and took to dancing in the streets in their joy. There are now, as part of the festivities, dramatic costumed performances which depict St George slaying the dragon – even though he doesn't appear in the Helston dragon legend.

Other spring fairs and festivals

There are numerous other springtime traditions, some better known than others.

Cuckoos and cuckoo days

For those who live in the countryside, one of the markers of the arrival of spring has traditionally been the sound of the first cuckoo of the year. Over the years, there has been a plethora of suggestions about whether it is good or bad luck to be the first to hear the cuckoo, and these often have regional variations. You may have heard your own.

Nineteenth-century workers would often stop work on hearing the first cuckoo, claim the rest of the day as a holiday and go off to the local inn to celebrate. This custom was known as **Wetting the Cuckoo** or sometimes **Cuckoo Foot-Ale**.

Members of the parade wear coloured ribbons and carry cuckoo effigies and puppets.

On the final Saturday of April, the West Yorkshire town of Marsden holds its annual **Cuckoo Festival**. All of the traditional springtime elements are there, with morris dancing, a maypole, storytelling and duck races. Central to everything else, though, is the cuckoo parade. A procession, accompanied by musicians and dancers, makes its way down the High Street. The members of the parade wear coloured ribbons and carry cuckoo effigies and puppets.

An old myth from Marsden tells that originally the townsfolk believed that if they could keep the cuckoo in the place it was first heard, then it would remain springtime all year round. To do this, they tried building a wall around it, but just as they reached the final course of stones, the cuckoo flew away. No matter how hard you try, you will never outwit nature.

There are a number of cuckoo festivals around the country. Different dates in April have been claimed as **Cuckoo Day** including 14 April in Sussex, 15 April in Hampshire and

20 April in Worcestershire, among others. These dates are generally connected with traditional local fairs.

Ram roasts

Spring fairs would take place across the country, including ram roasts. Modern roasts tend to be charity fundraisers: Kingsteignton in Devon has a well-established one at the end of May, while the one organised by the scouts in Cheadle, Greater Manchester has become their biggest charity initiative. Many people believe that traditionally the ram roast may have stemmed from animal sacrifices made to the Celtic god Bel at Beltane (see page 29). It is said that the offering of the ram at Kingsteignton, which led to the traditional annual roast, was an attempt to end a devastating drought. However, if you are familiar with the spring weather in Devon, you will know this seems unlikely!

Wrestling competitions

As well as large amounts of food and drink, music and dancing to enjoy, there were often sporting events at spring fairs. Wrestling competitions were popular and some areas such as the Lake District still have traditional wrestling competitions today. At other fairs, this has been replaced by the somewhat more flamboyant and performative entertainment of 'professional' wrestling.

Wormcharming

Moving beyond the confines of the fair, some more unusual outdoor sporting events take place in spring. In early May, at Blackawton in Devon, you can enjoy – and maybe even take part in – the **International Festival of Wormcharming**.

This is a more recent event, having been first planned by Dave Kelland in 1983. After a wet Sunday afternoon sampling a beer or two in the local pub with a friend, Dave found himself caught short on the way home. Making use of a nearby field, he observed how a number of worms surfaced from the ground while he was ... watering. Dave, or maybe the beer, decided that this would be a good idea for a competition and the rest is history.

Over the years, the competition has been developed into a popular festival, in the hope that it will continue for generations to come. Perhaps, in a couple of centuries, people will look back and wonder about the origins of this custom, in the same way we do about many ancient spring traditions. Folklore is a constantly changing and adapting area.

Should you want to take part, here are the rules. Teams or individuals are

You are first granted a five-minute 'worming up' phase in order to try and encourage your worms to the surface.

each given a plot of land, marked out as a 1 metre square. You are first granted a five-minute 'worming up' phase in order to try and encourage your worms to the surface. You are not allowed to dig or fork the ground, and neither can you put anything considered hazardous on it. Otherwise, any technique is fair game, from water sprinkling to paddling, to dancing and all points in between.

Teams are encouraged to compete in fancy dress and there is a competition for the best, as well as the most, worms removed from your square in the 15 minutes following the worming up.

Cheese rolling

What is arguably now a globally renowned annual spring sporting tradition, and one that continues to defy safety rules, is the **Cooper's Hill Cheese Rolling** at Brockworth, near Gloucester.

If you haven't witnessed this event (either in real life or online), it is pretty much what you might expect. A large 'wheel' of Double Gloucester cheese, weighing around 3 kilogrammes, is released from the top of the hill and large numbers of participants charge down after it in an effort be the first to the bottom.

Nobody ever beats the cheese, but the first to arrive does get the wheel (or whatever is left of it) as a prize.

You may want to think twice before considering entering as a competitor. Cooper's Hill is extremely steep, reaching an angle of up to 60 degrees in some places, and once you start your descent there are few ways to stop. Minor injuries are common, and more serious ones also quite possible. In 2023, the winner of the ladies' race learned of her success in the medical enclosure, having finished unconscious.

The first time that the Cheese Rolling appears in a written record is in 1826, in a letter to the Gloucester town crier, but it already refers to the fact that the tradition has been going on for a long time. The practice of scattering cakes and biscuits undertaken by the Master of Ceremonies before the event may hark back to the usual blessing of the land before the growing season.

Nobody ever beats the cheese, but the first to arrive does get the wheel (or whatever is left of it) as a prize.

If you want to observe or take part in the Cheese Rolling, it now takes place on Spring Bank Holiday Monday. Be prepared for the fact that the tradition has not been officially organised for some time, and you do so at your own risk. A barrelling cheese can be quite heavy at speed!

Mother's Day

Much like the Hallowe'en customs later in the year, some aspects of **Mother's Day** have been imported to Britain from America, where it is celebrated on the second Sunday in May, rather than the UK's fourth Sunday in Lent. In the United States, the tradition was established by Philadelphia resident Anna Jarvis in 1907, as a celebration of mothers and motherhood. In the UK, we have conflated this idea with the Christian **Mothering Sunday**, but traditionally it is not the same thing.

The church celebration of Mothering Sunday finds its origins in the Roman Catholic custom of mid-Lent Sunday. Worshippers from the outskirts of parishes would make their way to their 'Mother Church' for a service, which was then followed by much eating, drinking and merriment. The day was once known as Refreshment Day, recounting the biblical story of the feeding of the five thousand.

> *How did we move from this family tradition to the more commercial recognition of motherhood that exists now?*

Some examples of the old custom of **Clipping the Church** take place on Mothering Sunday. One can be found at the Church of St Helen in Whitley Chapel, Hexhamshire, in Northumberland. The custom involves members of the parish joining hands in a circle around the perimeter of the church in a celebratory embrace.

Into the 17th century, it was customary for servants and other young workers to be granted permission to visit their parents on Mothering Sunday. On the day before, the mother of the household would prepare a meal, which traditionally consisted of the hind quarters of a lamb, served with mint sauce and accompanied by suet pudding, sea kale, cauliflower and wheat furmity. Furmity was a popular dish in medieval times. It was also known as frumenty, and consisted of wheat boiled in milk or broth to make a kind of porridge.

The meal would be accompanied with homemade wine, and this would be followed with a large, rich simnel cake – a type of fruitcake, well baked and sugared and beautifully decorated. The daughter of the family, who was often working away from home as a domestic servant, would make this cake using ingredients provided by her employer.

So how did we move from this family tradition, which arose as an offshoot of a religious celebration, to the more commercial recognition of motherhood that exists now? This was simply because Mothering Sunday became confused with Mother's Day by American servicemen who were stationed in Britain during the Second World War. And never one to miss an opportunity, retail did the rest.

April Fools' Day

In contrast to Mother's Day, April Fools' Day remains far less commercial, but is still observed both by individuals and, increasingly, by media outlets and large businesses.

The tradition of April Fools' is fairly ably summed up by an 18th-century folk rhyme:

The first of April some do say,
Is set apart for All Fools' Day;
But why the people call it so
Nor I, nor they themselves, do know ...

In other words, we don't know! Some suggest that the tradition stems from the raven that flew from Noah's ark to look for land in the Christian version of the flood myth. Others connect it to the calendar change and the vernal equinox. The custom is also thought to come from the 'end of winter' celebrations in Roman times. Here's another possibility to consider ...

In Scotland, an April fool is sometimes referred to as a 'gowk'. This is Scots slang for a cuckoo, the bird whose celebration day we examined earlier (see page 48). The cuckoo is symbolic of someone who is a little simple. Scottish author Robert Chambers, who compiled the famous 19th-century *Book of Days*, makes mention of this in the tale of the 'Wise Fools of Gotham'.

One party made themselves busy fencing off a small tree so that the cuckoo in its branches could be kept captive from the Sheriff of Nottingham.

Gotham is a village in Nottinghamshire (completely unconnected to Batman), with a population of around 1,600 people. An area of the land known today as Cuckoo Bush Mound is the site where the tale is said to have unfolded. King John, the story goes, was once heading for Nottingham and on the way was going to pass through the meadow at Gotham. The villagers there thought that if the king walked over a piece of land then forever afterwards it would be designated as a public right of way, and they did not want to lose their valuable meadow land.

Therefore, they came up with a plan in order to prevent the king from crossing their boundary.

The king would always have servants riding ahead to clear the way for his progress. The plan saw all the villagers feigning stupidity and presenting themselves as a village of fools. Some were trying to drown an eel in the village pond. Some were discovered rolling cheeses down a hill (presumably more safely than at Cooper's Hill, see page 52) so that they would end up at Nottingham market. And one party made themselves busy fencing off a small tree so that the cuckoo in its branches could be kept captive from the Sheriff of Nottingham. This is what gave its name to the piece of land.

At the time that this happened, madness was believed to be contagious and so the king's servants returned and advised the party not to cross through Gotham, for fear that they would all become mad themselves. By this trick, the 'Wise Fools' in Gotham kept their land safe.

Whether they are marking traditional or religious calendar dates, commemorating important historical events or celebrating the return of greenery after a barren winter time, it is heartening that there are a multitude of spring customs still taking place around the country. Morris dancing, fairs and carnivals will all continue into the summer months. And so, now, shall we.

Meteorological summer:
1 June to 31 August

Astronomical summer:
Summer solstice (near 21 June) to
autumn equinox (near 23 September)

There are flowers enough in the summertime,
More flowers than I can remember –
But none with the purple, gold, and red
That dye the flowers of September!

'September' by Mary Howitt (1799–1888)

Summer

From the Welsh celebration known as Gŵyl Awst to the election of a mock mayor in the Oxfordshire town of Abingdon-on-Thames, from the Ould Lammas Fair in County Antrim to the World Stinging Nettle Eating Championships in Dorset, and from Scotland's Ceres Highland Games to the Chester Mystery Plays in Cheshire, as spring moves into summer it is a time of excitement throughout Britain.

The traditional landscape changes. The early signs of growth begin to flourish and mature; the new life of plants and wildlife grows and develops; everything around us becomes lush and verdant.

Many traditional celebrations still focus on giving thanks, sharing joy and making merry.

In days gone by, before the assistance of modern farming methods, those tending the land worked hard to ensure that there would be good harvests to see communities through the dark winter nights. The summer months represented the polar opposite of what was to come, and many traditional celebrations still focus on giving thanks, sharing joy and making merry. The long path of the sun across the sky gave people more time to be outside participating in these activities – both working in the fields and celebrating. One of the most important traditional times for celebration took place on the longest day, **Midsummer**, to mark the **summer solstice**.

Midsummer and summer solstice

It is clear that this time of year was significant to our ancestors from the arrangement of monuments such as Stonehenge in Wiltshire, where the rising of the sun aligns with the Heel Stone at the summer solstice. English Heritage recognises the importance of this to modern practitioners of older ways and allows free access to the site on this date. Thanks to modern

technology, this rising of the sun over the monument is now streamed live around the world. Not only does this allow more people to share in the celebrations remotely, but it has also cemented the summer solstice in the minds of many through the pictures and videos on social media.

Because the sun is at its height on the day of the summer solstice, for ancient pagan beliefs it symbolises a goddess who is with child and a sun god who is at his most virile. Neopagan and Wiccan followers celebrate a festival called **Litha** at Midsummer. This is not an extant ancient tradition but is part of the reconstruction of the Germanic pagan calendar, deriving its name from the Anglo-Saxon names for the two months which we would now identify as June and July. Litha celebrations borrow from the Midsummer practices of various cultures.

Fires and beacons

Much like Beltane in spring (see page 29), Midsummer Day also has an association with fire. Bonfires would be lit at this time to ritually amplify the sun's energy. There are still some fire festivals that continue this custom today.

Across Cornwall on 23 June – St John's Eve – you can observe Midsummer fires, known locally as **Tansys Golowan**, being lit. Although the summer solstice, when these would have traditionally been lit to mark the longest day, is a moveable date, it is likely that the lighting of the Cornish fires was moved slightly and fixed on this date to coincide with church calendar celebrations.

THE MANY VIRTUES OF ST JOHN'S WORT

With St John's Day being 24 June, the plant which bears his name – St John's wort – is most definitely associated with Midsummer. As well as being efficacious for mental health, and to improve ardour, this plant has very strong associations with protection. As early as the 13th century in England, we can find references to its use as a repellent for evil demons who were said to find its smell and presence disgusting.

St John's wort was widely used in Scotland for protection against witchcraft, as this translation of a verse from the Hebrides shows:

St John's wort, St John's wort,
My envy whosoever has thee,
I will pluck thee with my right hand,
I will preserve thee with my left hand,
Whosoever findeth thee in the cattlefold,
Shall never be without kine [cows].

St John's Eve is unusual for being one of the few dates that celebrates the birth of a saint rather than their death. In terms of the solar cycle and the Bible, this balances the birth of Christ six months later. In St John's Gospel, referring to the birth of Jesus, John the Baptist says, 'He must increase, but I must decrease.' This could be seen to directly corollate with the sun's presence in the sky diminishing between this time and the winter solstice. Bonfires were frequently lit on St John's Eve in honour of the saint, and were also believed to drive away evil spirits and witches. It makes sense, therefore, for the Cornish fires to have been relocated to this date.

Tansys Golowan takes the form of the lighting of beacons, starting at the furthest point in the south-west at Land's End. Fires are lit one after the other, until the last beacon close to the border with neighbouring Devon is reached. Flowers and other plants are tossed into the flames, and prayers are said at each beacon, often in Cornish.

At the modern revived festival of **Golowan**, which lasts for nine or ten days and takes place in the Penzance area of Cornwall towards the end of June, there are now a number of street processions. It has, in fact, grown to become the second largest street festival in the UK, and some traditional elements can be found in its music, spectacle and dance. Highlights of the festival are **Mazey Eve**, when the Mayor of the Quay is elected, **Mazey Day** and **Quay Fair Day** (Friday to Sunday respectively).

Mock mayors

The Mazey Eve election in Penzance is similar to another custom that takes place in Abingdon-on-Thames, Oxfordshire. The Saturday closest to the summer solstice (around 21 June) sees the annual **Election of the Mayor of Ock Street**. Rather than being the formal town mayor, this election is for a 'mock' mayor who also acts as the squire of the local morris dance side.

The tradition of electing mock mayors used to be common. The role was theoretically one intended to hold the real mayor to

account on behalf of the parishioners, but in practice was a parody of the pomp of real mayoral positions, and an excuse for a good party. Revivals of mock elections can be found around Britain, but the Mayor of Ock Street is one of two long-standing traditions, with the other being at Kilburn in North Yorkshire.

You have to be resident in Ock Street, or nearby, in order to vote in the election, but there is plenty to watch as a bystander. Morris dancing takes place around the town from noon until dusk. As the sun goes down, the newly elected mayor is borne on a litter of flowers to the market place for the final dance of the day.

At this event, there is also a chance to see the **Horns of Ock Street**, used by the Abingdon Traditional Morris Dancers. At an ox roast in the town's market in 1700, a fight broke out between boys from Ock Street and those from another part of the town, as to who would get to keep the horns. Ock Street were the victors and now they proudly carry a cast-iron ox's head and horns on a pole whenever they dance.

Morris dancing takes place around the town from noon until dusk.

Back in Cornwall, also present at the modern Mazey Eve celebrations is **Penglaz, the Penzance 'obby 'oss.** This is a style of hobby horse similar to those found in Wales known as the Mari Lwyd (see page 161), constructed using a horse skull on top of a stick and carried by a dancer covered with a cloth skirt. These hobby horses were also used in Cornwall for mumming traditions around Christmas time (see page 158).

Trees and plants

Trees and plants are important to Midsummer celebrations. Those found near wells or sacred water sources would often be decorated with coloured cloths. These strips of cloth of rag are known as **clooties**, from the Scots term for cloth, and are tied ritualistically, often to support a healing prayer or similar. It is important, if you choose to do this, to ensure that anything left is biodegradable and will not harm the tree in any way.

Mistletoe used to be cut at Midsummer as well as in the winter. As a parasitic plant, it can often be found in oak trees, which many considered sacred. In pagan symbolism, the summer is the time of the **Oak King** before he passes power back to the **Holly King** in winter.

An annual custom found only in the village of Appleton Thorn in East Anglia demonstrates this important link between trees and folklore. Taking place on the third Saturday in June, the festivities are centred around a hawthorn tree growing in the centre of the village. The tree allegedly grew from a cutting taken from the Glastonbury Thorn, which legend says sprouted from the staff of Joseph of Arimathea, the biblical figure said to be responsible for the burial of the body of Jesus.

The ceremony at Appleton is called **Bawming the Thorn**, with 'bawming' meaning 'decorating'. This is undertaken by children from the local primary school, who process to the tree where they sing the Bawming Song and perform a circle dance reminiscent of maypole dancing. The custom is then followed by a celebration that includes market stalls, refreshments and music performances.

Like many such customs, the current version is a revival of something much older. The original ceased at some point in the 19th century and was then revived in the inter-war period before being re-established in its current form in the 1970s.

The Appleton Bawming Song, which is sung to the traditional folk tune 'Bonnie Dundee', contains a couple of verses that mention the sacred trees and plants of summer celebrations in times past:

The oak in its strength is the pride of the wood,
The birch bears a twig that made naughty boys good,
But there grows not a tree which in splendour can vie
With our thorn tree when Bawmed in the month of July.

Kissing under the rose is when nobody sees,
You may under the mistletoe kiss when you please;
But no kiss can be sweet as that stolen one be
Which is snatched from a sweetheart when Bawming the Tree.

Both the rose mentioned here, and the feast of St John the Baptist, figure in a rather more formal annual custom that takes place in London each June.

In London in the 14th century, the English knight Sir Robert Knollys owned a house near the church of All Hallows by the Tower, on what is now Seething Lane. While he was away on business, his wife Constance bought the land opposite their house, which had previously been used for threshing wheat (and from where Seething Lane gets its name), and created a rose garden there. When she built a footbridge from their house to the garden, the City of London granted permission for it to be used only on the payment of an annual tithe of one red rose upon the feast of St John.

A formal ceremony to present this rose – **Knollys Rose Ceremony** – first took place in 1381 and can still be seen every June, performed by the Company of Watermen and Lightermen, one of the historic London guilds. After a rose is cut from the garden, which still exists on Seething Lane, the bloom is placed on an altar cushion from the church. A procession of members of the guild and clergy from the church then take the flower to Mansion House where it is presented to the Lord Mayor of London.

Another ancient London custom takes place on the first Thursday after 4 July. This is the **Vintners' Procession**, which marks the election of a new Master for the Vintners' Company – the guild of wine merchants established in 1363.

The procession passes from the Livery Hall, where the election takes place, to the nearby Church of St James Garlickhythe where a special service is held. As the company passes between the two locations, a Wine Porter moves in front, sweeping the path with a broom made of birch twigs. This is symbolic of a necessary task during medieval times as the streets were strewn with dirt and waste. In a similar fashion, medieval vintners and clergy would have carried nosegays – posies of flowers which smelled far more pleasant than the streets on which they were walking. As well as still wearing Tudor apparel, those in the modern procession also still carry small bunches of flowers.

Rushes were also used to scent the air and to provide a renewable floor covering for cleanliness. The summer months, and June in particular, see a number of **rushbearing ceremonies** taking place in churches, predominantly in the north of England. Modern versions of the ceremony sometimes vary from the original depending on the location.

Before the introduction of flagstone floors brought an end to the practice as a necessity and turned it into a custom, churches would have plain earth floors. These did not do much to prevent smells from pervading the building, particularly as the deceased were often buried inside, as well as outside in the churchyard. Some people will tell you that the practice of interring wealthy people inside the church led to the phrase 'stinking rich', but sadly this isn't true!

The summer months, and June in particular, see a number of rushbearing ceremonies in churches predominantly in the north of England.

In order to offset the issue of bad smells, naturally pleasant-smelling rushes would be scattered on the church floor. This had the added benefit of providing the church with insulation and helping to keep the congregants warm. The custom was known as rushbearing or rush strewing and it would usually take place on important feast days in the church calendar, as the rushes would require renewing periodically.

There are a number of rushbearings at churches throughout Cumbria during June and July. In the village of Grasmere, for example, the rushes for the floor are borne on a white sheet held by six girls in green and white costumes. Others in the procession carry rushes and flowers fashioned into different shapes. Local children at this rushbearing are given a piece of the famous Grasmere gingerbread for taking part.

In some areas, where rushes are now less plentiful than they used to be, hay is used in their place. This is usually the case at the ceremony that takes place at St Peter's Church in Barrowden, Rutland on 29 June, the feast day of the saint to whom the church is dedicated.

A rather different use of plants takes place at the **World Stinging Nettle Eating Championships**, held on the Saturday before the summer solstice. People from all over the world travel to Marshwood in Dorset to compete, although you may want to think twice before entering yourself. Stinging nettles need to be boiled to remove the hairs if they are used in nettle soup or other recipes. If you eat them raw, as this competition demands, then they cause your tongue to swell and turn an alarming shade of purple or black.

A rather different use of plants takes place at the World Stinging Nettle Eating Championships, held on the Saturday before the summer solstice.

You'll also need to eat quite a lot of them to stand a chance of winning. In 2024, the men's champion got through the leaves from 116 feet worth of stalks to claim the trophy. The women's champion, defending her victory from the previous year, munched through 64 feet.

The tradition of competitive nettle eating started in the 1980s. The only assistance provided to competitors is a glass of cider, which they can drink or dip the nettle leaves in to soften them.

Summer fairs and ceremonies

The summer months are supposed to be blessed with good weather and so traditionally many fairs take place at this time of the year. These fairs would often be where officials would test the quality of local products to ensure that the public were not being short-changed. This would include tasting ale and weighing bread, to make sure that the correct measures were being used. Ceremonial customs remembering this legal practice can still be found at many summer fairs.

A particularly fine example of this tradition can be found in the Devon town of Ashburton, where the **Ancient Ale Tasting and Bread Weighing Ceremony** takes place every year on the third Saturday in July. In Anglo-Saxon Britain, local law was the responsibility of a reeve: port-reeves for towns and shire-reeves (from where we get the term 'sheriff') in more rural areas. Because Ashburton is one of very few towns that was given permission to retain its ancient court in the 1970s when the Justice Act was implemented, it still appoints a Portreeve.

However, the role today is symbolic and forms part of local charitable events.

Nowadays the ceremony in Ashburton is more fun than formal, with a jester, medieval musicians and other entertainment alongside the bread and ale inspections. Bakeries in the town often produce the most elaborate loaves that are then weighed. These are auctioned off later to raise money for local charities and often fetch a high price. The ale tasting comprises an elaborate series of events, as each pub is visited and the required two tankards of ale for tasting are offered.

The procession arrives at a pub and finds the door shut. Petals are scattered on the threshold and the Court Marshals knock to gain entry. Once the ale is produced, the ale tasters assess its quality using a method which legend insists was the usual routine.

Once the ale is produced, the ale tasters assess its quality using a method which legend insists was the usual routine.

As well as being tasted, the ale is poured over a wooden bench and then the taster, who wears medieval leather breeches as part of his costume, sits on the bench. If the ale is bad, then it will cause the leather – and therefore the taster – to stick to the bench. Once the ale has passed its inspection, the Portreeve presents the landlord or landlady with a sprig of evergreen to hang over the door so that everyone will know that the quality of their product is assured.

A similar, although perhaps slightly more formal, fair and

procession can be found at Bromsgrove in Worcestershire, generally on the Saturday closest to Midsummer. As in Ashburton, an ancient court is still in place here, not with any legal powers but tasked with charitable work and the preservation of historical tradition. Following a procession of the court members in their full regalia, ale and meat are ceremonially tasted, bread is weighed and leather is checked.

In the Suffolk town of Bury St Edmunds, it is cake rather than bread that features in a traditional annual event. The Thursday before 29 June is the date of the annual **Cakes and Ale Ceremony**.

Jankyn Smyth was alderman of Bury St Edmunds in 1423 and was known for his philanthropic work. On his death in 1481 he left instructions in his will that a Mass should be held in the town each year, along with a bequest of money to provide cakes and ale. A charity was set up to administer his wishes, and over time it has been used to found almshouses in the town, and is thought today to be the oldest endowed charity still operating.

The Cakes and Ale Ceremony begins with a service at St Mary's Church where children from the local schools sing. Everyone is welcome to attend and afterwards invited guests move to the Guildhall. Here, the cakes and ale are served. The latter is a special ale brewed locally, which is used for a toast to Jankyn Smyth in remembrance of his generosity.

A few **'white glove' fairs** can be found in the summer season around the country. These tend to be fairs where a royal charter was granted at a very early stage. A white glove, which is symbolic of a ceremonial glove or might originally have been the

mayor's actual glove, is placed on the top of a pole decorated
with garlands of flowers and foliage. This is carried at the head of
a procession of musicians and dignitaries before being placed
somewhere prominent for the duration of the fair.

The tradition dates back to an original point of law which

stated that while the 'glove was up' anyone who was attending the fair could not be arrested for debt. Hoisting the glove is a custom that is often associated with a **coin scramble**. As the glove is put into position, coins are thrown to the ground, which children try to collect.

Records show that an unusual number of thunderstorms would take place around the date of Ebernoe Horn Fair.

Originally at these fairs the coins would have been given by the gentry and heated until they were red hot before being thrown. Watching the poorer classes trying to gather them would have been a cruel source of entertainment. While the coins in scrambles today are obviously no longer heated, at the fair at Honiton in Devon, which takes place each July, they are still warmed in recollection of this custom.

On St James's Day, 25 July, a fair in Sussex recalls the traditional ram roastings that we explored earlier (see page 50). The **Ebernoe Horn Fair** is a mid-19th century revival of a custom that had been observed for hundreds of years before.

In the revived version of this event, the horns from the ram roasted during the day at the Ebernoe Fair were removed and presented to the highest scoring batsman in a cricket match that is held throughout the day. At the modern-day fair a trophy in the shape of a set of horns is used in place of the real ones.

Records show that an unusual number of thunderstorms would take place around the date of Ebernoe Horn Fair. This seems to have been a common enough phenomenon that the storms were regarded by local farmers as a sign that the harvest season would bring bountiful yields.

Gardeners would use the date of the fair as a marker to sow cabbages. This was a common practice with country fairs because their occurrence was a much easier way to mark the passage of time than actual calendar dates. In Devon, for example, **Honiton Fair** was used as the date when swedes should be singled (thinned) and kidney beans were never planted until after the revels took place at the village of George Nympton. This would have meant that the soil was in the best condition for growing that particular crop.

Gardeners would use the date of the fair as a marker to sow cabbages. This was a common practice with country fairs because their occurrence was a much easier way to mark the passage of time.

A traditional Horn Fair song is always sung at Ebernoe. It tells of a young man walking to the fair who is passed along the way by a woman on a horse who he tries to persuade to allow him to ride with her. It begins:

As I was a-walking one fine summer morn,
So soft was the wind and the waves on the corn.
I met a pretty damsel upon a grey mare,
And she was a-riding upon a grey mare.

The action of riding on a grey mare is connected with another summer fair which also has a song – possibly one of the better-known folk songs today. The event is **Widecombe Fair**, and so is the title of the song that tells of a group of men borrowing a horse. They all climb on with the intent of riding to the fair until, bearing so much weight, the horse dies while crossing the wilds of Dartmoor.

Tom Pearce, Tom Pearce, lend me your grey mare,
All along, down along, out along lee,
For I want for to go to Widdecombe Fair,
Wi' Bill Brewer, Jan Stewer, Peter Gurney, Peter Davy, Dan'l
*   Whiddon,*
Harry Hawk, old uncle Tom Cobley and all, old Uncle Tom
*   Cobley and all.*

The traditional fair at Widecombe-in-the-Moor in Devon is always held on the second Tuesday of September. It had humble beginnings in 1850 as a simple cattle market, but became increasingly successful and popular over time. Since it started, its run has been broken only by the Second World War, the 2001 foot-and-mouth epidemic, and the 2020 Covid-19 pandemic. The song and its tune have something of a contested history, starting sometime in the early 1800s, and originally not being associated with Widecombe Fair at all.

The offering at Widecombe Fair now makes it akin to a small country show, with arts and crafts, livestock competitions, folk music, specialist demonstrations and more. Traditional elements

A SPELL FOR BEAUTY

As well as being used for divining who a future partner might be, the yarrow plant was also used as part of a charm recited by women who wished to make themselves more attractive. This spell would have been done in early summer. Whilst gathering the yarrow, these words were spoken:

I will pick the smooth yarrow
That my figure may be more elegant,
That my lips may be warmer,
That my voice may be more cheerful;
May my voice be like a sunbeam,
May my lips be like the juice of the strawberries,
May I be an island in the sea,
May I be a hill in the land
May I be a star when the moon wanes,
May I be a staff to the weak one;
I shall wound every man,
No man shall wound me.

include terrier racing, which was introduced and replaced pony races in the 1980s during an outbreak of equine flu, and the tug of war that always closes the fair. The latter was an introduction made when the fair returned in 1945, at the end of the Second World War.

Always present at the event is someone dressed as **Uncle Tom Cobley** riding, as you would expect, a grey mare, while all the other characters walk.

Lughnasadh and Lammas

Roughly midway between the dates of the summer solstice and autumn equinox, the first day of August is important in the folklore calendar, as it marks the beginning of the harvest season. The terms Lammas and Lughnasadh are often used interchangeably, but it is important to try and draw a distinction between the two, as they derive from different belief systems.

Lughnasadh

Lughnasadh (pronounced 'loo-nah-sah') is an old Gaelic festival celebrating the coming of harvest time, which was celebrated across Ireland and Scotland. Its name derives from the god of the harvest – Lugh – and 'seanadh', the Old Irish word for assembly or gathering. Lugh has been described as the **Celtic Sun King**

but this is contested by some folklorists. Certainly he was known in Irish mythology as being multi-skilled and his festival was widely celebrated. August is a sacred month to this figure.

In terms of the symbolism at this time of year, the goddess is now seen as the **Grain or Corn Mother** with her daughter representing the grain, or seed, which will grow to make crops for the next year. The Grain Mother is depicted as heavily pregnant because she carries within her the seed that will form next year's Sun God.

At one time it was traditional to climb large hills or mountains at Lughnasadh and we still find this custom being enacted in some areas. The Welsh equivalent to Lughnasadh is a celebration known as **Gŵyl Awst**, when on 1 August people head off into the Bannau, the mountains that separate Glamorgan and Carmarthenshire, to walk to Little Van Lake. In Welsh lore, the **Lady of the Lake** would appear here on this date.

Modern pagan practices have subsumed Lughnasadh into the Wheel of the Year (see page 9), although it is sometimes conflated with the Christian festival of Lammas.

Lammas

Lammas comes from the Old English meaning 'loaf mass' and is a festival on the Christian liturgical calendar that takes many of its elements from the Lughnasadh celebrations. The loaves baked using the first wheat to be harvested are taken to church and blessed, and we still see this reflected in modern harvest festival services. This bread would, in the past, have also been used ritually to offer protection to the crops being harvested. For example, the loaf would sometimes be split into four, with each piece being placed in the four corners of the barn where the harvested crops were to be stored.

Once again, there are a number of summer fairs that mark this time of year. Said by some to be Ireland's oldest traditional fair, the **Puck Fair** takes place over three days in Killorglin, County Kerry, between 10 and 12 August. The Irish name for the fair,

Aonach an Phoic, translates as the 'fair of the he-goat' and this links the event with the old custom of going into the mountains.

Before the fair begins, a wild billy goat is captured from the nearby MacGillycuddy's Reeks mountains and is brought down into the town. The goat will be known as **King Puck** and it is ceremonially crowned in the town square by a girl from one of the local schools who is chosen as **Queen Puck**. This coronation marks the start of the fair.

Traditionally, the goat would have been put in a cage on top of a high stand for the duration of the fair, to 'oversee' events. Due to concerns around animal welfare, nowadays the goat is only displayed for an hour or two, and is looked after elsewhere for the rest of the festival. At the close of the fair it is released back into the mountains.

It is likely that, if the Puck Fair was originally connected with Lughnasadh, the goat was seen as a symbol of fertility. Much like the early spring traditions, fertility would be associated with the seed that would be sowed for the following year's crops. In the same vein, we find games at the Welsh **Gŵyl Awst festival**, which probably derive from the same beliefs. These include **Rhibo** where couples are thrown into the air by a group of men, and **Awr Ar Y Gwair**, which translates as 'an hour in the hay', and probably needs no further explanation!

Northern Ireland also has a particularly ancient Lammas fair, known unsurprisingly as the **Ould Lammas Fair**. This takes place on the last Monday and Tuesday of August in Ballycastle, County Antrim, and vies with the Puck Fair for being the oldest in Ireland. In the 1960s, parties from each of these two fairs visited their counterparts as guests. This did not go entirely to plan when the Killorglin party brought King Puck with them to visit Ballycastle. While making what was probably a much-needed stop in a pub, the goat escaped and evaded all attempts to recapture him, allegedly being left with a bullet hole in one of his horns as a permanent record. He never got to lead the parade that was planned for him.

Dances, plays and parades

Folk dancing and other public performances have always been a vital part of our cultural life. They serve as an expression of our identity, both in the present and the past, whilst bringing communities together as a shared experience.

Horns – not given as a cricket trophy nor sporting a bullet hole – provide a central focus for one of the oldest ritual customs still enacted in England. The **Horn Dance** at Abbots Bromley in Staffordshire takes place at the same time each year, but you'll have to concentrate if you want to work the date out successfully. The festivities take place on the Monday following the first Sunday after 4 September.

The dance is performed by a group of six men who carry large sets of reindeer horns mounted onto wooden heads. A pole at the bottom of the head allows them to be carried. The first dance of the day takes place at 8am at St Nicholas's Church, after

which the group spend the day dancing around the local area. When they are not being used for the Horn Dance, the horns are stored in the church, where they have been kept since the early 19th century. Prior to that, they resided at the Town Hall.

The dancers are accompanied by a musician and a young boy with a triangle – a role which seems to have been added at the beginning of the 20th century. Joining them are four more characters: a boy with a bow and arrow, a man dressed as Maid Marion, a Fool and a hobby horse. The hobby horse is not of the hoop type found at Padstow or Minehead (see page 32), but is of a type known as a **tourney horse**. The horse is worn a little like a skirt and held up by shoulder straps, in a similar vein to the fancy dress outfits that make you look like you are riding a dinosaur, for example.

There is no traditional tune for the **Abbots Bromley Horn Dance**. A mix of folk dance melodies and more modern tunes are used. Nor are there any specific steps used by the dancers, who move in a combination of simple circling and advancing and retreating rows.

The origin of the Horn Dance is unclear. It does appear to be very old, as the reindeer antlers used have been dated to the 11th century. These would most probably have been brought to the UK from Scandinavia as there were no reindeer in Britain at that time. The earliest record of the horns can be found in 1686, although a hobby horse performance is described a century earlier. It has been suggested that the dance was first seen in 1226, when it was performed as part of the fair held to celebrate St Bartholomew's Day, but there is no written evidence to support these.

It is possible that the dance was once a ceremony to bring good fortune for hunting, in much the same way that other rituals at this season looked to bring favour upon the arable crops. An alternative theory could be that in the Horn Dance we are seeing some remnants of a medieval play that was held in the summer rather than at the more usual Christmas time, with the dance being an integral part of the drama.

A more easily verified set of medieval plays can be found in the city of Chester in Cheshire. The **Chester Mystery Plays** date back to the 14th century; they were performed for two hundred years until banned under Queen Elizabeth I's anti-papism laws, and then revived for the 1951 Festival of Britain. They continue to be performed every five years.

At the time that the mystery plays were written, church services were conducted in Latin, which the majority of people could not understand. To overcome this, other methods were used to deliver the important messages of the Bible and the meanings behind them. Often, this would be through the use of religious art, but the monks of St Werburgh's Abbey, which is now Chester Cathedral, wrote the plays as another way of sharing the stories with the public.

The plays became so popular that they had to be moved from the confines of the abbey to enable everyone to attend. The individual trade guilds in the city took on responsibility for producing and performing one of the 24 plays. Some of these would be appropriate to the craft or trade that the guild represented. For instance, the Guild of Grocers, Bakers and Millers would perform 'The Last Supper'.

> *When the mystery plays were written, church services were conducted in Latin, which the majority of people could not understand.*

Plays would be performed in English and included plenty of humour to appeal to the 'common folk'. They took place on highly decorated wagons, which could be rolled through the streets to different locations, often accompanied by a procession of musicians, acrobats and clowns.

There are scripts surviving from a few English cities with mystery play cycles; the Chester scripts, with their near-complete texts, are the most valuable. The modern performances are large-scale community events and, being performed only every five years, are a popular feature of both the folk and arts calendars in the UK.

Large parades took place both at Midsummer and Midwinter in Chester, and were a tradition that grew out of the mystery plays. These were seen in the city for many hundreds of years, and featured musicians, dancers, acrobats and depictions of creatures from folklore and mythology.

The parades today recreate what these might have looked like, and usually include processional **giants** similar to those that would have been present in the early versions. Giant characters have appeared in public folk traditions across Europe for many centuries, with the earliest recorded in Britain being from Salisbury, Wiltshire, in the 16th century.

St Bartholomew's Day

While there may be little evidence to suggest that the Horn Dance at Abbots Bromley was performed on St Bartholomew's Day (24 August), other events do link with this date. One of these is the **Bartlemas Bun Run**, which appropriately takes place in the Kent town of Sandwich.

The Bun Run follows after a special church service which celebrates St Bartholomew's Founder's Day. It is said that in 1217 the town received a large sum of money, won in a battle at sea off the Kent coast. This money was used to build a chapel and hospital that were dedicated to St Bartholomew.

As a part of the service, a new Master of the hospital is elected from among the residents living in the almshouses to serve for the coming year, in a custom called **'pricking out'**. A list is written of all the eligible people, one of whom is chosen by the sticking of a silver bodkin into their name.

Once this formal ceremony is performed and the new Master has recited the traditional oath, the children get to participate in the Bun Run. When the race starts, the children run around the perimeter of St Bartholomew's Church.

The word 'race' is perhaps something of a misnomer; there is no first place and no last place. Every child who participates is given a bun as a prize and the adults in attendance are all presented with a traditional hard biscuit. These are a little reminiscent of the tradition of the Biddenden cakes (see page 25).

St Bartholomew doesn't fare quite as well in North Yorkshire, where he is burnt in effigy each August. Or is he?

Burning effigies

These days, the public burning of a figure is generally used as a form of protest, and of course in some cases this also happens through custom. The most obvious example would be the bonfires associated with Guy Fawkes Night on 5 November, a festival which derives from the holiday declared to celebrate the survival of King James I following the assassination attempt by Guido Fawkes and his fellow conspirators (see page 141).

In terms of the traditional year, burning in effigy is more commonly connected to the changing seasons, in celebration of the coming of spring and summer, or to give thanks for good harvests. In the Wensleydale village of West Witton, North Yorkshire, where the church is dedicated to St Bartholomew, the **Burning of Bartle** takes place on the Saturday closest to 24 August.

Participants and onlookers, of whom there are usually many hundreds, start to gather at dusk in preparation for the parading of Bartle's effigy. This is a figure stuffed with straw, not unlike the effigy that is cast into the sea at the culmination of the Hunting of the Earl of Rone at Whitsun (see page 36). The body is dressed in simple rustic clothing and the face is a mask with glowing eyes.

As the procession makes its way through the streets, there are frequent pauses (often conveniently situated at public houses) and a verse is recited detailing Bartle's alleged exploits before capture:

In Penhill Crags he tore his rags
At Hunter's Thorn he blew his horn
At Caplebank Stee he broke his knee
At Briskill Beck, he broke his neck
At Wadham's End, he couldn't fend
At Briskill End, he made his end
Shout, boys, shout.

This is delivered in local dialect for the most part. Once the parading of the effigy is complete, it is placed against a dry stone wall, stabbed and then set alight – Bartle really wasn't very popular.

But who does this effigy actually represent? This is somewhat unclear. We know that the custom goes back hundreds of years, but the origin story remains unknown. Suggestions include a giant who used to live in the area, St Bartholomew himself or one of his relations, and an unnamed livestock rustler who was captured hiding out in the nearby Penhill Crags.

This is all tantalisingly vague. Older stories of giants are generally transformed in folklore into stories involving the **Devil** after they were adopted by the church during medieval times. Any connection to St Bartholomew seems unlikely, as saints were generally venerated or remembered in positive events and not in this way, particularly as there are a number of buildings dedicated to Bartholomew. And the robber tale lacks detail: sometimes he was caught in the 18th century and sometimes he wasn't; sometimes he had been stealing pigs and sometimes it was sheep.

Whatever the story behind the Burning of Bartle, the custom has become firmly established, and has grown into a weekend of family events, games and crafts.

Another annual custom that used to involve an effigy, although this has changed slightly in recent years, is a ritual fire held at Whalton in Northumberland. This has taken place on 4 July for a number of years, and is known as either the **Whalton Bale Fire** or **Whalton Baal Fire**. A bonfire is lit, and there are displays of dancing by local children and morris dance teams, as well as music and general celebration.

There is some disagreement over which of the two names is correct and it seems likely that the variation could have come about through different pronunciations of the name: Bale Fire might suggest what was used as fuel; whereas Baal seems more likely to connect with more ancient fire festivals and customs.

As a god, **Baal** was an aspect of nature who was locked in a battle with **Mot**, the Mesopotamian god of death. Baal's victory would herald seven years of fertility for the land, whereas if Mot was victorious there would be seven years of famine and poor conditions. If this sounds familiar, then you are probably thinking of Joseph's dreams that he described to Pharoah, as recorded in the Bible's Book of Genesis (or on stage if you are a fan of musical theatre).

These beliefs are paralleled in the spring traditions of welcoming the return of life over winter death. As we saw in the Celtic Beltane fire festivals (see page 29), people would jump through fire in order to cleanse and purify themselves, and to invite fertility. At the Whalton Fire, there used to be a tradition of jumping through the flames, but this is no longer practiced.

A straw effigy known as a **Kern Baby** also used to be ritually cast into the fire. Although this no longer happens, it does connect the custom further with ancient fire celebrations. A Kern (corn) Baby is a human-shaped doll, which was fashioned out of some of the last corn to be gathered at the end of the harvest as a way of giving thanks for the crops, and the figure would then be used as an offering for the following year.

This links with many similar customs at the end of harvest, which we will look at in more detail as we move into autumn.

A large sculpture of a corn doll, inspired by photographs of the original Kern Baby taken in the 19th century, is now erected each year, but is not consigned to the flames.

Water sports and customs

With the more favourable weather conditions over the summer months, festivals and sporting activities on water are frequent events. Some of these are quite formal in nature. Others are a little more unusual.

In London, the River Thames is a focus for a number of water-based competitions. Some are easily recognised. The first races pitting the students of Oxford with those of rival university Cambridge took place from the second decade of the 19th century and have evolved into the annual **Boat Race**. Not long after, in 1839, **Henley Royal Regatta** began, and grew into a five-day event.

Less well known is the traditional **Race for Doggett's Coat and Badge**, but this is probably the oldest race in any sport that has been running continuously since its inception. The race was started by an actor, Thomas Doggett, in 1715. Doggett was born in Ireland before settling in London, where he made his stage debut in 1691 and worked through to his retirement in 1713.

He founded the race to commemorate King George I's accession to the throne.

Every July the race is contested between the watermen and lightermen of the River Thames, whose guild is responsible for organising the ceremonial presentation of a rose to the Lord Mayor of London in memory of the rent owed from the garden belonging to Sir Robert Knollys (see page 69).

Watermen used to be responsible for transporting people along the Thames, with the lightermen being those who moved the goods from the land to larger vessels, using barges called lighters. Today they both serve different, but equally important, roles on the river. The period of training and examinations runs for five years, and it is those in their first year who compete in the Doggett's Coat and Badge.

A number of coracle regattas take place during August. Many date from the 19th century or are modern revivals of older races.

The type of boat used has changed a number of times over the years, with single sculls currently being provided for the competitors. The race winners are sometimes offered prestigious ceremonial duties for members of the Royal Family and other dignitaries. Indeed, there is much pageantry surrounding the race day itself.

A number of coracle regattas take place during August. Many of these date from the 19th century, or are modern revivals of the older races. August Bank Holiday Monday sees the annual **Ironbridge Coracle Regatta** on the River Severn and the

Coracle World Championships are held each year in Shrewsbury, Shropshire on Saturday of the week that includes 19 August.

Coracles are small, one-person boats, which are designed to be carried on a person's back; hence they are particularly lightweight. They are thought to date back to pre-Roman times and were often used by those hunting or gathering food. But they have also served more unusual purposes. At Shrewsbury, the home of the world championships, in the middle of the 20th century it was one man's job to strike out in a coracle and retrieve footballs from the town's pitch that had ended up in the river.

Staying on the water, but moving back to the River Thames, the ancient tradition of **Swan Upping** takes place in the third week of July each year. This ceremony, the modern version of which is predominantly used to check on the health and welfare of London's swan population, dates back to the 12th century.

Over a five-day period in July all the swans on the river are checked and if they are young cygnets their ownership is determined.

All mute swans in Britain's waters, without markings to signify otherwise, belong to the Crown with two exceptions. The Worshipful Company of Vintners (with whom we are already acquainted) and the Worshipful Company of Dyers still also hold rights that were granted to them historically, and which they retained in the

16th century when the rights of all other landowners were revoked.

Over a five-day period in July all the swans on the river are checked and if they are young cygnets their ownership is determined. The **Royal Marker of the Swans** is rowed by members of the Company of Watermen and Lightermen.

Nowadays, all the birds are ringed. In the past, the swans that did not belong to the Crown had their bills nicked with a sharp tool to indicate ownership – one nick for the Dyers Company and two for the Vintners. The name of an old coaching inn in the City, once located in what is now Gresham Street, the Swan With Two Necks, is probably a corrupted form of 'the Swan With Two Nicks'. The inn closed in 1860.

There used to be many customs related to blessing stretches of water, and the sea in particular. While many of these are no longer extant, others are still practised, such as the annual **Blessing of the Sea** at Hastings, East Sussex. A religious service for all faiths is held on the harbour, along with the singing of hymns related to the sea. The tradition used to fall on Ascension Eve (39 days after Easter), but now takes place in August.

Another of these traditions is the **Blessing of the Waters** at Mudeford in Dorset. This takes place on Rogation Sunday, which in the Christian liturgical calendar is the fifth Sunday after Easter, and so can theoretically fall in either spring or summer. It is often around the end of May. On this day, the vicar is taken out into the quay in a rowing boat, from which he delivers a short blessing and throws a cross into the sea. Both events raise money for the Royal National Lifeboat Institute.

As church ceremonies, these blessing customs can be traced back to 15th-century Italy, from where they spread across Europe and into North America. According to the story, a bishop was travelling across the sea on the Feast of the Assumption (15 August, the date on which many of these customs still take place), when a storm blew up. He offered up prayers and threw his bishop's ring into the water, whereupon the storm abated, and he was able to continue safely on his journey.

Greek Orthodox Christians perform similar blessing ceremonies at Epiphany, the end of the 12 days of Christmas. Some of the sanctified water is collected and used to bless homes, farmland and livestock. It is also used to drive away the Kalikantzaroi, malevolent goblins from the folklore of southern Europe, which live underground for most of the year but emerge at Christmas to cause all sorts of mischief.

An ancient water tradition also connected with Ascension or Rogation takes place each year at Whitby in North Yorkshire. A hedge, constructed from hazel and willow, must be woven by two men on the east bank of the River Esk, and then staked in the water offshore, at which point a horn sounds and the men issue the cry, 'Out on Ye!' The hedge, which must be completed by 9 o'clock in the morning on Rogation Wednesday, must withstand three tides without coming apart or falling down. If it does not survive, then tradition dictates that disaster will fall on the town.

The **Whitby Penny Hedge** custom is unusual in that it is not a revival of an original tradition. It is said to trace back to the 12th century and since then the hedge has been built every year except one: in 1981 the tides were so high that the usual site was completely submerged.

As with most old customs there is a legend that surrounds it, and then a more likely explanation. The legend holds that in 1159, a hermit who lived in the local area was beaten to death by hunters because he was trying to protect some wild boar that they were pursuing. The huntsmen were captured and tried but were pardoned for the crime on the condition that they must build the hedge each year using a single knife, and that their descendants must continue to do so.

> *As with most old customs there is a legend that surrounds it, and then a more likely explanation.*

The knife that the men had to use, the court stated, must cost them a penny and this is one derivation for the name Penny Hedge. An alternative suggestion is that the name is a contraction of 'penance hedge' in view of the court stipulation. This story is almost certainly a later concoction; in some versions the hermit is a monk, which gives the story potential papist overtones.

A more likely explanation is that the Penny Hedge originally maintained an old manorial boundary, similar to the beating of the bounds (see page 38). It is likely to relate to a feudal ceremony from the area known as the **Horngarth**, which was a fence surrounding farmland adjacent to the Monastery at Whitby.

Food races and events

While many summer boating traditions paint a picture of the calm, idyllic British countryside at this time of year, some sports – water related and otherwise – have entered into folklore perhaps not for their formal regalia or long-standing history, but because they are more unusual. Here we look at those with a food theme.

This is certainly true of the (usually) annual **Yorkshire Pudding Boat Race**, which has taken place in Brawby, North Yorkshire since 1999. The concept was the work of local artist Simon Thackray, who specialises in unusual arts installations and live events, and the name of the race is now a registered trade mark.

The boats used in this race are actual Yorkshire puddings, a traditional accompaniment for roast beef made using a batter of flour, milk and eggs, which is baked in the oven. The puddings are large enough to seat a single rower, and are coated with several layers of yacht varnish to prevent them from absorbing water and sinking or breaking apart.

The boats used in this race are actual Yorkshire puddings.

The Yorkshire Pudding Boat Race has been staged relatively regularly since its inaugural event, although some years have been missed. On the years where it hasn't taken place, one of the ingredients could have been used for another unusual annual summer sport.

The **Egg Throwing World Championships** take place each

year in late June in the Lincolnshire village of Swaton as part of their vintage fair. Despite the fine array of old vehicles, traditional crafts and other activities on show, press coverage has ensured that the Egg Throwing now takes top billing.

Once again, this competition is relatively recent having been started in the mid-2000s, although it does claim to have much older traditional roots. The rules are quite simple. Teams are made up of two people, a 'tosser' and a 'catcher'. They start 30 feet apart, and the tosser throws the egg to the catcher, who must catch it without it breaking. A successful catch means that the team can move further apart and try again.

The current world record stands at 309 feet and was achieved by a New Zealand team in 2016. As well as the main competition there are other categories that people can try, including **Russian Egg Roulette**, which involves two players and six eggs, five of which are hard boiled and one of which is raw. The eggs are selected at random and broken on the player's forehead. It's easy to guess who is judged the loser!

Organisers claim that the competition came from an event that took place at an abbey in the village in the year 1322. The abbot there kept chickens and used to give villagers one egg each on a Sunday if they attended the church service. As nobody else had chickens at this time, this almsgiving can be seen as more of a bribe.

In the year in question, the story goes that the river flooded, and the locals of Swaton were unable to reach the church. In order to distribute the alms, the monks stood on the river bank and threw the eggs across to their parishioners.

Sad to say it is highly unlikely that there is any truth to the story. The Swaton Eau, the river that runs through the area, is some distance away from the main church around which most people would have settled. Historical records are also very scant for any monastic buildings in the Swaton area. But all good traditions, even new ones, should have a backstory that is at least plausible.

The perfect complement to the Yorkshire Pudding Boat Race, though, is undoubtedly the **World Gravy Wrestling**

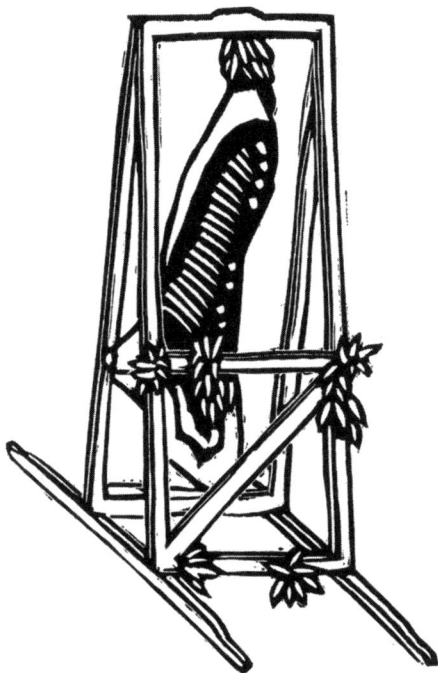

Championships, staged at Rossendale in Lancashire every August. Although it only began in 2007, this competition has already entered into folklore, no doubt due to the action often featuring in newspapers, on TV and online.

The Gravy Wrestling Championships are a charity fundraising event, supporting East Lancashire Hospice and other beneficiaries, which are chosen by those taking part. A pool filled with Lancashire gravy is the arena in which wrestlers 'fight', with points awarded for costumes, entertainment value and sometimes even their ability to wrestle.

The flitch is a side of bacon awarded to any married couple who can prove that over the period of a year and a day they have 'not wisht themselves unmarried'.

A much older tradition involving food, although with no sporting competition this time, takes place in July each leap year in the Essex town of Great Dunmow. These are the **Dunmow Flitch Trials**. The flitch referred to here is a side of unsliced bacon that is traditionally awarded to any married couple who can prove that over the period of a year and a day they have 'not wisht themselves unmarried again'. A jury of six unmarried women and six unmarried men preside over the participating couples.

Some details about the history of this custom are uncertain, but we do know that it has a long history. Geoffrey Chaucer makes mention of the tradition in 'The Wife of Bath's Tale' and even earlier, in 1362, author William Langland includes it in his narrative poem *The Vision of Piers Plowman*. Neither of these titles give any kind of detailed description of the custom, so we can assume that it was well known at that time.

The most often repeated story about the origin of the Dunmow Flitch tells how Robert Fitzwalter, the feudal baron of Little Dunmow, set up the annual Flitch Trial as a condition for his bestowing land to a local priory. This idea was popularised by Victorian writer William Harrison Ainsworth who published a novel entitled *The Flitch of Bacon* in 1854.

In Ainsworth's telling, the tradition came about because Fitzwalter and his wife dressed as peasants after their first year as a married couple, and visited the priory to ask for a blessing. The prior gave a flitch to the couple and Fitzwalter then subsequently decreed that the same thing should be done for any couple who could prove they had not regretted their marriage after the same length of time. It is this novel that was responsible for reviving the Dunmow Flitch Trial, as so many traditions were in the 19th century. The custom had previously died out some time after 1751, according to surviving records of couples who were awarded a flitch.

In order to defend themselves couples have to kneel on a stone before the jury, where they face rigorous questioning intended to avoid awarding the flitch. Those who are successful are carried away on a special chair on the shoulders of traditionally dressed bearers. Originally there were two pointed kneeling stones, but these were removed before the custom was revived. The original oak carrying chair is still preserved at the priory.

Although unusual in that it still takes place, the Dunmow Flitch Trial is not unique. There was a custom at Wychnor in Staffordshire that was almost identical and was similarly said to have been a condition of a deed of covenant. A wooden carving of a side of bacon, and the oath the couples had to swear in this version, can still be found at Wychnor Hall. References to flitches of bacon alluding to a similar practice also exist in other areas of Europe.

It seems likely that these trials come from much earlier customs used by the church in order to instil in people the importance of the sanctity of marriage. Many stories and traditional practices in folklore today have these origins; in the case of the flitch, this probably dates back to the Saxon period.

Ceres Highland Games

More traditional games and pursuits can be found at the oldest free games to be held in Scotland: the **Ceres Highland Games**. These are staged on the last Saturday in June and date from 1314, when they were established to honour local men who fought at the Battle of Bannockburn. This is recorded in Scots verse:

For this is June's great gala-day!
When men rin wud and youngsters play
The day that marks the grand return
Of Ceres men frae Bannockburn!

The games have always been held on the village green, which is today called the **Bow Butts**. This is the location, it is said, where Scottish knight Sir Robert Keith taught local men the bowmanship required for battle.

The day will usually begin with a procession of bands, and this is followed by the games themselves, which are a busy mix of track and field events, cycling and strength tests common to many of the Scottish Highland gatherings, such as the caber toss and shot put. Displays of traditional Highland dancing and piping are common, along with a unique event – the throwing of the **Ceres Stane**.

The Ceres Stane is a large, heavy rock that can usually be found in the local pub, but which is transported to the games each year. The one currently in use dates from the beginning of the 20th century, but it is possible that the event itself began in 1332, when there is a reference to a 'heavy rock' that was 'fetched from the bed of a mountain stream'.

Pixie Day

At the other end of the country, also taking place in June and close to Midsummer's Day, is the annual **Pixie Day** at Ottery St Mary in Devon. Pixie Day in its current form was put together in the middle of the 20th century, but it is thought to have its roots some 500 years or so earlier.

Belief in fairies and pixies lingered for a long time in rural parts of the country, such as Devon and Cornwall and parts of

Wales, as well as Ireland and Scotland. This was especially the case in places where people lived in more isolated areas, such as on the moors.

Local stories say that pixies used to live in the area around Ottery St Mary, but that the arrival of humans forced them to leave. In particular, they were driven away once the church was built, as it is a common part of fairy lore that fairies have an aversion to the ringing of church bells. To get their own back, the pixies stole into Ottery and kidnapped the bell-ringers, taking them back to the moors and concealing them in a cave, from where they eventually managed to escape and return to town.

This folk tale is memorialised in the Ottery St Mary Pixie Day celebrations, which see the children of the town dressing as pixies. After the festivities of a traditional fair in the afternoon, the children run through the streets in pursuit of the church bell-ringers who play their part in recreating the story. They are caught and imprisoned in a specially designed cage, known as the **Pixies' Parlour**, in the town square before they too make their escape.

Across the length and breadth of Britain, from Scotland with its Highland Games to the Ottery St Mary pixies and all points in between, the customs and festivities of summer are a mix of celebrations taking place under warm, sunny skies, giving thanks for the conditions that will lead to a good harvest and a time of plenty as the year advances.

From here, we move into the gathering-in of those crops before the nights draw in, the verdant landscape changes to russet and gold, and autumn approaches.

Meteorological autumn:
1 September to 30 November

Astronomical autumn:
Autumn equinox (around 23 September) to
winter solstice (around 22 December)

I love the fitfull gusts that shakes
The casement all the day
And from the mossy elm tree takes
The faded leaf away
Twirling it by the window-pane
With thousand others down the lane

'Autumn' by John Clare (1793–1864)

Autumn

The end of the summer saw the first harvests of the year being gathered in, with all of their associated traditions and customs. As the first weeks of autumn pass, the countryside becomes a blaze of colour as the leaves turn and fall. Today, with the ease of mechanisation, harvest time happens quickly. In times gone by this would have been a community event, as the produce would sustain those people through the long winter days ahead.

In summer we looked at the custom of electing mock mayors (see page 65). In Cornwall, this was a common practice at the time of the autumn equinox. Revived ceremonies can be found today at both Penzance and Polperro, connected with the Guldize festivities (see page 112). In these towns in times past the mock mayor was celebrated as **King of the Feast**, putting them more in line with the medieval **Lord of Misrule**. The Lord of Misrule, or Abbot of Unreason as the appointment was called in Scotland, was an elected commoner who was put in charge of organising revelries over the Christmas period – often these took the form of wild drunken parties.

Autumn Equinox or Mabon

The autumn equinox falls towards the end of September, and the main focus of celebrations is on giving thanks for the harvest. More recently, this festival has also become known as **Mabon**, named after the mythological Welsh god who was the son of the **Earth Mother Goddess**. The festival draws heavily on ancient harvest celebrations and traditions, much like its spring equivalent of Litha. Its modern name only came into use in the 1970s, when the Wiccan practitioner Aidan Kelly included it on his Wheel of the Year. Apples are a frequent symbol of Mabon festivities, being associated with the late harvest time.

Harvest festivals

Many are familiar with the term Harvest Festival through the services that take place in churches and this time of year has always been seen as one of celebration. Traditionally, it takes place on the Sunday closest to the **Harvest Moon**.

The Harvest Moon always rises very soon after sunset; it provides a period of bright moonlight for several nights, meaning that in the days before electricity crops could be gathered much later into the night.

Festivals to give thanks for the harvest have also been important in other cultures around the world. They might take place at different times of the year, or in different ways depending on the crops or the continent, or even hemisphere, but they all share the same message – one of gratitude.

This message would be conveyed through prayer, as it is in church services today, and also through ritual sacrifice. The last of the corn to be cut would often be fashioned into a dolly or a token called a 'neck'. This final cutting was a time of great ceremony, which can still be seen today in the vestiges of the custom of **Crying the Neck**.

The Harvest Festival in Cornwall is known as **Guldize**, coming from the Cornish language term *Gool dheys*. This means 'the feast of ricks', ricks being the old method of stacking sheaves in the fields to dry. Crying the Neck ceremonies still take place in many parts of Cornwall and neighbouring Devon during the harvest period. As the last bunch of corn is cut, it is lifted into the air by the person who cut it, with the declaration: 'I 'ave 'un! I 'ave 'un! I 'ave 'un!' The crowd then asks what it is the reaper has, to which the reply comes: 'A neck! A neck! A neck!' Then there are cheers of celebration, both for the corn and for the farmer.

A feast for the whole community might be thrown at a harvest celebration and some landowners would do the same in return for their farmhands. In England, this was often known as **Harvest Home**. The corn dolly, or neck, would form the centrepiece at the table

As the last bunch of corn is cut, it is lifted into the air with the declaration: 'I 'ave 'un! I 'ave 'un! I 'ave 'un!'.

and afterwards would be safely stored, sometimes hanging in the farmhouse or sometimes in the local public house. The following spring it would form a ritual sacrifice to the land, being ploughed into the soil as an offering before the sowing of new crops took place.

At one time the Harvest Festival was known as **Horkey** or

Hoakey in some parts of the country. This term seems to have come into use in the Middle Ages and did not fall out of fashion until the 19th century. Horkey, or its many various alternative spellings, derives from the word 'hooky' which was shouted as part of a harvest enactment from the 16th century. One of the farm labourers would play the part of lord of the manor, dressing in fine clothes and trying to solicit money from people in the crowd, who would shout 'Hooky, hooky' as the cart was brought in from the fields.

There seems to be only one remaining example in Britain of a somewhat more formal celebration, the **First Fruits Ceremony**, which takes place earlier in September in Richmond, North Yorkshire, as the harvest begins. This is a civic ceremony where a sack of grain from the new harvest is brought by a farmer for inspection by the town mayor and the local miller. Following the original format, the corn is looked over and hopefully declared good, and then toasts are drunk in recognition of the crops.

Michaelmas

In the Christian calendar, **Michaelmas** – 29 September – marked the official end of the harvest. On this date, in a similar fashion to the election of the mock mayors but with rather more importance, one of the farm labourers in each community would be elected to the position of **reeve**. In summer, we heard about the duties of the modern-day reeve at Ashburton in Devon (see page 72). Nowadays the reeve is responsible for planning

charitable events and fundraising, but traditionally the role was somewhat different and not especially desirable.

The reeve had to ensure that all the labourers in the community who were responsible for the growing and harvesting of the crops were making a sufficient contribution. They would also collect rents from people living in cottages owned by the local landowner. If the rent collected was not the amount demanded, then the reeve would be liable to make up the difference.

Michaelmas was one of the quarter days, all of which were, and still are, tremendously significant in the pagan calendar. It is not surprising then that there are so many customs and beliefs associated with this time.

As well as the end of harvest, folk traditions tell us that Michaelmas is when we should stop foraging for blackberries. This was the date on which the Devil was said to have fallen from heaven, landing in a blackberry bush. In his anger, he spat on the blackberries (or worse!) rendering them unfit to eat.

This is one of those stories that emerges from observation of the natural world, as so many of our folk beliefs do. As the weather changes, the fruit of the blackberry tends to become fly-blown and shrivelled, meaning that it is not worth picking.

Michaelmas foods

Food is an important part of customs connected with significant festival dates and while you might not want to eat blackberries there are other things you might like to try, such as Michaelmas cake or stubble goose.

In both Scotland and Ireland, the baking of a **Michaelmas cake** was traditional and many people still practise this custom today. In the Hebrides, for example, the cake is known as a Struan Cake, or *Bonnach Struthan*. In similar fashion to the traditional cake on Mother's Day (see page 55), the Struan would be baked by the eldest daughter of the family. It was representative of the fruits of harvest time.

The Michaelmas cake made in Ireland had a tradition connected to it a little like the hiding of a coin in a Christmas pudding, only with a different purpose. When it was offered to a large gathering, a ring would be added to the cake batter before it was baked. The belief was that the guest whose slice of cake contained the ring would, if they were single, be likely to marry within the year.

It was considered to be important to eat goose at Michaelmas

– also known as the Feast Day of St Michael the Archangel. This particular bird was known as a **stubble-goose** because it was fattened for the table by being put out to eat the wheat stalks that remained standing in the ground after the harvest had finished.

'Eat a goose on Michaelmas Day, Want not for money all the year', went a verse on the subject.

In Ireland, the eating of the stubble-goose would take place in honour of **St Patrick** and the role that he played in saving the son of an Irish king. A legend told that the prince choked on a bone at a royal feast but was saved after the king prayed for St Patrick to intervene. Henceforth the king ordered geese to be slaughtered every Michaelmas.

The same tradition, but without the accompanying legend, took place in Scotland, where the custom was said to bring good luck for the year ahead. 'Eat a goose on Michaelmas Day, Want not for money all the year', went a proverb on the subject.

Goose fairs

Because this was considered to be a good time to eat goose, markets selling geese were common during autumn and a couple of significant examples still survive, although their format has changed over time.

Nottingham Goose Fair takes place in early October and now runs for ten days, having previously spanned five. Although you won't find geese there any more, the fair has run for many centuries and is thought to pre-date the royal charter granted to the city in 1284.

Prior to the calendar change of 1752, which placed it in October, the market took place in Nottingham on 21 September and was known as **Goose Fair Day**. As many as 20,000 geese would be driven to Nottingham from up to 50 miles away. Their feet would be painted with tar and sand forming a sort of 'shoe' to give some protection over the long walk.

The modern fair, which is organised predominantly by showmen, brings together one of the country's largest assemblages of fairground rides and attractions and is quite a spectacle.

Even older than the Nottingham fair is the **Goosey Fair**, which is held in the Devon market town of Tavistock. This has its origins as far back as 1105, when the monks of Tavistock Abbey were granted permission by King Henry I to hold a market each Friday. A little later, in 1116, this was extended to a three-day event. This second grant bestowed upon the town the status of a 'port', referring not to any maritime links but to its being a trading centre. A port-reeve was then appointed to organise the fairs and markets.

As well as the geese being transported to the town from around Dartmoor, local farmers would also drive cattle and sheep down from the moors, so the event was a large-scale livestock market. This fair originally took place on Michaelmas Day, but due to the calendar change was moved to the second Wednesday of October.

Autumn feasts and fairs

An ancient feast still takes place each year at Houghton-le-Spring, near Sunderland, on a Saturday in early October and was originally another Michaelmas tradition. The **Houghton Feast** dates back to the 12th century and spans several days, although the main day is focussed on the Saturday.

Now you can expect to see a carnival, musical entertainment and fairground rides as part of the festivities. However, up until 1938, horse racing also formed part of this event, although it doesn't seem to have been quite as lawless as those held on Lingay (see page 129) – the people of Houghton used their own horses!

Folklore has the event being founded by Bernard Gilpin, Rector of the Church of St Michael and All Angels in Houghton-le-Spring, possibly as a celebration after he returned to the parish following his arrest on heresy charges during the reign of Queen Mary I. This, however, cannot be the case as Gilpin served the parish in the 16th century and we know that the feast is much older.

Where Reverend Gilpin did play a part is in the introduction of the **ox roast** that now forms a central part of the Saturday events. It is believed that he would donate a bullock or a pig to the parish each year for the feeding of the poor, as well as providing food each Sunday through the winter for his parishioners.

The Houghton Feast is a particularly long-standing example, but there are still a number of other traditional fairs taking place through the first part of autumn. The first Saturday in October sees the annual **Blackberry Fair** at Whitchurch in Shropshire, which celebrates the end of the blackberry season.

The provision of food by prominent members of the community would often be the highpoint of fairs like this. This was the case at Marldon in Devon when, in the late 19th century, a local businessman named George Hill would provide a huge apple pie each year for the village fête, organised by the local church. The pie would be brought on a donkey cart and distributed to everyone attending.

The fair is presided over by an Apple Pie Princess, the local equivalent of a Carnival Queen.

Marldon Apple Pie Fair was revived in 1958 and now takes place on the first Saturday of September. In reference to the original fête from 1888, the apple pie still arrives on the back of a cart, which is pulled by a donkey – or local school children if the donkey is unavailable. The fair is presided over by an **Apple Pie Princess**, the local equivalent of a Carnival Queen.

Apples formed a significant part of the harvest at this time of the year, and when we see references to the 'fruits of the harvest' this makes the connection to orchards. In the 1990s, the festival of **Apple Day** was created in order to promote both the consumption of apples and the health of our orchards. Since then, we have seen an increasing number of new events connected with apples and apple traditions taking place at orchards and other heritage sites around the country.

Perhaps one of the biggest of these is the **Big Apple** at Much Marcle in Herefordshire, which is held on the first Saturday and Sunday of October. Apple experts are on hand to identify varieties, alongside demonstrations of apple pressing, cider-making and tastings.

The apple has appeared in many religious traditions over the centuries, often as some form of mystical or forbidden fruit. But sometimes it can be difficult to pin down the folklore, as up until the 17th century the word 'apple' could be used as a generic term for any foreign fruit that was not a berry. Tomatoes were called 'love apples' when they were introduced into Europe. Cucumbers have been referred to as 'earth apples' in some Old English writing and in other languages the term is applied to potatoes. Oranges have been called golden, or Chinese, apples.

Even nuts were sometimes referred to as apples. As we saw earlier, we definitely wouldn't want to go gathering nuts in May, as they wouldn't be very nice. The traditional date of **Nutting Day** was 14 September, when foraging for nuts would take place. Couples liked to go nutting in the woods together, which often led to more babies than usual being born in June.

A week later, 21 September, was known as **Devil's Nutting Day**. In line with the folklore surrounding blackberries, this was the date when gathering should stop, as the Devil would appear, wanting his share.

Autumn crops and hops

Another harvest brought in at this time of the year was the hop harvest, with hop flowers being used as part of the beer brewing process. Similar to Apple Day, a modern-day custom in Kent has developed in celebration of the county's connection with this crop. The **International Hop Festival** takes place on the first weekend of September in Faversham. Street entertainment, morris dancing and singing are all part of the fun on the

A Hop Queen and attendant princesses carry a bower covered in hops, and morris dancers perform.

Saturday. The following day, a member of the local clergy will bless the beer that is brewed. A barrel is rolled through town to the church, where it is placed at the altar ready for the service to take place.

At nearby Canterbury, a similar celebration happens on the second Saturday of September. The **Hop Hoodening** here was established as a folk event in 1957 and has since become an annual tradition. Once again there is a church service, which takes place at Canterbury Cathedral, in order to give thanks for the hops. A **Hop Queen** and attendant princesses carry a bower covered in hops, and morris dancers perform both inside the church and around the town. 'Hoodening' refers to an East Kentish tradition of a ritual play that included a hobby horse and would usually take place at Christmas.

Harvest characters

At the end of September each year the North Yorkshire town of Whitby hosts a tradition called **John Barleycorn Must Die**.

This ceremony takes its name from a traditional folk song which personifies the crop of barley and its path from sown seed to brewed drink through the character of John Barleycorn, describing how he is thrown into the ground, buried and declared dead, and yet rises again:

Then they let him lie for a very long time
Till the rain from heaven did fall,
Then little Sir John sprung up his head
And soon amazed them all.
They let him stand till midsummer day
Till he looked both pale and wan.
And little Sir John he growed a long beard
And so become a man.

They hired men with the scythes so sharp
To cut him off at the knee.
They rolled him and tied him by the waist,
And served him most barbarously.
They hired men with the sharp pitchforks
Who pricked him to the heart.
And the loader he served him worse than that
For he bound him to the cart.

In the ceremony at Whitby, John Barleycorn is represented by a large effigy that is carried through the town in a procession, accompanied by drummers and costumed attendants, before being taken to the local brewery. Here, the effigy is pulled apart in a ritual dismemberment, accompanied by music and projected images. Following this, a piñata in the shape of a man is beaten with sticks until the torso breaks apart and concealed gifts are revealed. This reflects the thrashing (or threshing, the words are interchangeable) of the barley before it could be used for the brewing process that would ultimately lead to the prize beer, which everyone would drink.

While some customs may be lost or fall out of favour, others continue to be born. A new harvest tradition that has developed in the 21st century at Carshalton, to the south of London, has its roots embedded in the harvest celebrations of old. This is the **Carshalton Straw Jack**, a perambulatory figure built around a wooden frame and covered in the last straw from the harvest.

The Jack is carried around town, accompanied by drummers and musicians in costume, from lunchtime until early evening on the first or second Saturday of September. At the end of the day the Jack is taken apart and the straw is handed out to onlookers to take home. In earlier versions of the ceremony these bundles would be ritually burned in a brazier in the garden of the pub where the procession terminates.

Although the ceremony is clearly related to harvest celebrations, reinforced by accompanying characters such as the Scarecrow, the Reaper Man and the Corn Dollies, it is also based very firmly on the **Jack in the Green** celebrations that take place around May Day. These springtime ritual processions were originally formed by chimney sweeps and would have featured musicians and dancers, along with other finely-dressed participants. The centrepiece of these was the Jack, a wicker or basketwork frame, as at Carshalton, but decorated with greenery and flowers, rather than straw.

Most of the original Jack in the Green ceremonies, unlike modern revivals that are found around the country, were based in London and the surrounding counties. Many writers have suggested that the Jack holds direct associations with the **Wild Man of the Woods** or the legendary figure of **Robin Hood**, or with the more widely recognised **Green Man**. However, this is difficult to substantiate.

The earliest reference to the Jack in the Green appears to come from the 18th century. Prior to this, what would be called a Green Man was someone acting as a 'whiffler': in the 16th century he would precede processions to clear away the crowds. The Green Man would often dress like a wild man, or a horned god, but would sometimes be covered in foliage, not unlike a Jack.

As well as being similar in design to the Jack in the Green, the Carshalton Straw Jack resembles one or two other straw costumed characters from British folklore customs, most notably the **Whittlesea Straw Bear** in Peterborough, Cambridgeshire. These customs tend to be associated with Plough Monday (see page 187), the first Monday after twelfth night, and so look ahead to spring planting rather than the harvest.

Bell-ringing

Not all customs stem from major seasonal events of national significance. Sometimes they can emerge from very individual events on a local level. Such is the case with a bell-ringing tradition that still takes place on 7 October each year in the Hampshire village of Twyford near Winchester.

One night a local man named William Davis was making his way back to the village on his horse after dark when he became lost. On the air he heard the familiar sound of the bells of the Church of St Mary, but the noise was not coming from the direction he would have expected. He quickly reined in his horse, only to realise that had it not been for this warning the two of them would have galloped over the edge of a nearby quarry.

The story goes that William Davis was so grateful for this lucky escape that he left money to the church in his will for the purpose of funding an annual ringing of the bells in memory of the role that they had played that night.

The money was used up some time ago, but the ringing of the **Lost in the Dark Bells** still takes place. The bells are rung early in the morning and then again at around 7pm. There is also a meal provided for the bell-ringers on the day.

In 2022, the bells of St Mary's were restored, and in some cases replaced, and were blessed, as is the Church of England tradition, in a special evening service before being rehung. The eight bells were bedecked in flowers, ribbons and greenery, and lined up in the aisle of the church for the occasion.

Lost customs

Sometimes there is no obvious reason for a custom to be established. It may be that something happens spontaneously that people enjoy; over a period of time that event is repeated and evolves into something more elaborate. The event becomes a tradition and either endures or slowly fades away.

These sorts of events can turn into a reason to celebrate or have a party. And while this is not necessarily a bad thing, a number of traditions were lost during Victorian and Edwardian periods, when they were considered to be unruly, morally problematic or went against the teachings of the church. A number of these customs, as we have seen, have been brought back into the folklore year during periods of revival.

The group would spend the rest of the day roaming around the countryside with no real purpose. They would head for ponds, ditches and hedges in order to become wet and muddy.

One example of this is **Ganging Day**, which used to take place each Michaelmas at Bishop's Stortford in Hertfordshire, and in the surrounding villages. A large gathering of men, and a smaller number of women, would come together to choose one of their number to be the leader.

Once the choice was made, the group would spend the rest of the day roaming around the countryside with no real purpose. They would head for ponds, ditches and hedges in order to become wet and muddy. In the villages, the group would call at each pub and request a gallon of ale, which the landlord had to supply to them. Each time the group met a member of the public, they would 'bump' them. This was not so much a small nudge, but rather seizing them by the arms and using them to barge into another person.

You can imagine that those taking part in Ganging Day were

not terribly popular. Perhaps in recognition of this, the tradition also ensured that, once day turned to night, no one from the ganging group was allowed to stay in town; they had to walk into the countryside to continue their partying.

There appear to be no records offering an origin for this strange tradition, but it was still well established in the 18th century. It seems that the custom disappeared during the 19th century; it is likely that the wild partying was too much for Victorian sensibilities and the church authorities, and it ceased for much the same reason as the Hunting of the Earl of Rone (see page 36).

The Lancashire town of Eccles is the home of the famous Eccles cake. A round pastry, rather than a cake in the normal sense, this currant-filled delicacy is an important part of the British culinary landscape. History suggests that the Eccles cake was originally produced to celebrate the feast day of St Mary, which previously had an associated festival known as the **Eccles Wakes**.

The Wakes probably began in the Norman period and were held over four days, beginning on the first Sunday of September. In their original form they were purely a church celebration, but then other elements began to be added and the Wakes became more of a public spectacle, with feasts and entertainment as well as competitive events. Donkey racing, cock fighting and fiddle-playing competitions are among the activities recorded.

Although some respectable church rituals still formed part of the Eccles Wakes, including a rushbearing tradition (see page 70), the event's reputation for being drunken and riotous spread, and in the end the local authorities decided to intervene. They petitioned the government and the Home Secretary banned the Wakes in 1877.

Sporting events

Horse racing used to be a popular pursuit at Michaelmas although this tradition is now less common. The sport was recorded on the Isle of Lingay, one of the Western Islands of Scotland in the 18th century, with a couple of traditions attached to it.

The **Michaelmas races** would be held on the beach at the end of each September. It was decreed that for this day only, people could not be prosecuted for stealing a horse, providing it was to be used in the race and was returned afterwards none the worse for wear. This undoubtedly led to many dubious measures to try and secure the best horses on the island.

People could not be prosecuted for stealing a horse, providing it was to be used in the race.

A number of other sporting disciplines often featured in traditional community gatherings, and still do, including foot races. In Deeside, Scotland, the **Braemar Highland Gathering** takes place on the first Saturday of September each year. Here, foot races have been regularly held since 1832.

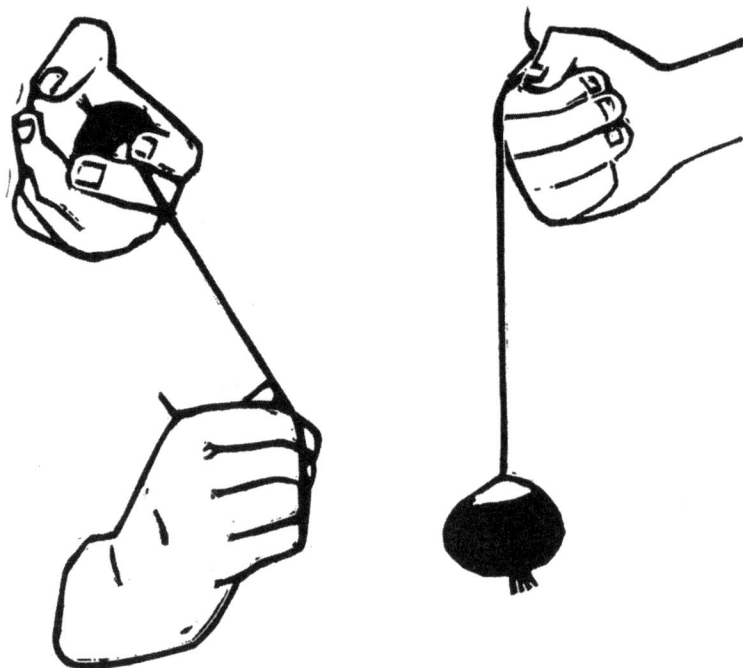

While still running in the form that it took in the early 19th century, the Braemar Gathering goes back much further. Some 900 years ago, Scots folk would come together to appoint their monarch as **Chieftain of the Gathering**, and traditional games would take place. All of the usual elements of Highland Games can still be found here today, including highland dancing, caber tossing and piping displays.

Some sports of the autumn season are a little more unusual than others. With the proliferation of horse chestnuts falling at this time of the year, it is natural to find that the **World Conker Championships** are held on the second Sunday of October. Now taking place at the Shuckburgh Arms pub in Southwick,

Northamptonshire, the original competition was staged on the village green at nearby Ashton, and dates back more than 50 years.

The World Conker Championships involve some very specific rules that you will not find in a standard school playground battle. Players are given nine strikes to try and break their opponent's conker by hitting it with their own, taken in turns of three each. Conkers are supplied pre-threaded and the length of that thread, or thong, is measured so that it is always the same. These rules are designed to ensure fairness and equity for all the players.

However, Britain was rocked by news of potential cheating at the 2024 championships! David Jakins, aged 82, was declared the champion for the first time, having been a competitor since 1977. But scandal came about after his opponent, Alastair Johnson-Ferguson, accused Jakins of cheating by substituting a metal conker for the one allocated.

While Jakins did have a metal conker in his pocket, which he insisted he was carrying for 'humour value', it was unlikely that he would have been able to defy the rules and substitute it for the official conker. Jakins was cleared of the accusation with the chairman of the event rejecting the claims of cheating, commenting that the metal conker clearly did not look the same as a real one.

Many people, of course, carry lucky charms, and perhaps that was Mr Jakins's motive in this instance. But any luck soon wore off, because in the match between him and the women's champion, Kelci Banschbach, David Jakins lost.

The story made the national press as one of those great examples of British eccentricity, and this led to a response from another conker championship – because there are more than just the one ...

The **Peckham Conker Championships** take place at roughly the same time of year in the south-east London borough, but are very different. Described as no-holds-barred and 'conkers-meets-*Fight Club*', the charity fundraiser positively encourages cheating, with conkers being baked, painted with super glue and more.

A more sedate competition is held in October at Long Clawson in Leicestershire and shares similar rules to the World Championships; however, in the quarter of a century that they have been staged to date, no scandals have occurred.

The game of conkers is first mentioned in 1821 in the memoirs of the English poet, and former Poet Laureate, Robert Southey, although at this time snail shells were used. The first reference to the horse chestnut being employed as a weapon comes from 1848 on the Isle of Wight.

Perhaps even more unusual as a sporting event are the **World Black Pudding Throwing Championships**, held on the second Sunday of September in Ramsbottom, Lancashire. The tradition is said to celebrate in friendly terms the perceived rivalry between the counties of Lancashire and Yorkshire, through the medium of their regional foods.

Yorkshire puddings (of a normal size, not like the ones in Brawby, see page 100) are piled up on a high platform. In a manner similar to a fairground tin-can toss, or coconut shy,

NINETEENTH-CENTURY
WEST COUNTRY LOVE SPELL

Upon All Hallows' Eve, write
these words upon an apple:

Coamer, Synady, Heupide

Then say:

*I conjure thee apple, by these names written on thee,
that whosoever shall eat thee shall burn in my love.*

competitors try and knock them down by throwing three black puddings at them.

The competition has been running since the 1980s and some people say that it stems from the fact that, during the Wars of the Roses in the 15th century, soldiers from the two counties resorted to firing food at each other when they ran out of actual ammunition. This story is, of course, apocryphal: cannons might have fired grapeshot, but they did not use grapes.

Samhain and Hallowe'en

Turning back to the major Celtic festivals which form the basis of so many of our traditions, we move to **Samhain** (pronounced 'sow-inn'). This festival marked the end of the harvest when crops were stored for the winter. The cycle of birth and growth is finished, and Samhain denotes the point of death.

Thus, Samhain is also known as the **Feast of the Dead** and is traditionally a time to remember those who have passed and honour the ancestors that came before. The boundary between the world of the living and the dead was said to be easier to pass through at this time of the year, meaning that the spirits of the dead would be able to cross and join those still living.

Ritually and symbolically, Samhain marks the start of the darker half of the year. However, this is not seen as a morbid time, because in nature death is followed by renewal. The

Sun God is given back to the land where he remains until the winter solstice that marks the time of his rebirth.

The transition from ritual festival to the modern celebration of **Hallowe'en** is controversial for some. There is an argument that the modern Hallowe'en has become imposed upon the three days of feasting for Samhain which starts on 31 October.

In fact, there are also divided views about Hallowe'en itself, also known as **All Hallows' Eve**. At one time, All Hallows' was celebrated in May before moving to 1 November, this date being established by Pope Gregory III in the 8th century. This is a Christian festival where prayers would be offered prior to the feast day of All Hallows, also known as **All Saints' Day**.

All Saints' Day does not refer only to those who have been canonised as such, but rather to all of the departed who have faithfully followed the teachings of Jesus Christ. In the Catholic church, the day is followed by **All Souls' Day** (2 November), which was devoted to honouring those souls who were in purgatory because they died having committed minor sins and had not yet moved to the realm of heaven.

The boundary between the world of the living and the dead was said to be easier to pass through at this time of the year.

Accounts of Samhain practices, especially from Ireland, describe how fires would be extinguished on the night of 31 October before being ritually re-ignited the following day. This process was symbolic of the New Year in ancient times.

TWO RITUALS FOR SAMHAIN

At Samhain, collect seven twigs. Each one represents something that you want to say goodbye to or leave behind. Bind them together with something green and bury them in the soil.

There was a long-standing belief that fairies lived in the branches of hawthorn trees. Hawthorn was seen as providing a gateway or bridge to the spirit realm and so at Samhain you would stand the best chance of seeing or communing with fairies if you sat beneath its branches.

There was a custom across much of Britain, and particularly in the north of England and in some parts of Scotland, of lighting bonfires at Hallowe'en, as there was at many of the ancient festival times. Bonfires were seen to be valuable for ritual protection and to ward off any evil spirits who might be roaming the land. Rolling on the ground near to the bonfire and inhaling smoke brought purification.

There are many fire festivals around this time of year which hark back to these old Celtic roots. In Edinburgh, the Beltane Fire Society has organised a Samhain (or Samhuinn) parade each year since 1995, as well as another at the end of April since 1988. Both of these are usually held at Calton Hill.

The **Edinburgh Samhuinn Parade** tells the story of summer being overthrown by the forces of winter through costumed dance, performance and music. The **Summer King** is banished and the **Winter King** takes his place, with the whole process being overseen by the **Cailleach**. In Gaelic myth, she is a crone goddess, known as the divine hag or the **Great Mother**, who is associated with the coming of winter, creation and destruction.

In Halton, Cheshire, over All Souls' Day weekend there have been revived performances of the ancient tradition of **Souling** or **Soulcaking** since the beginning of the 21st century.

Souling is an old house-visiting custom, which often involves singing a traditional song in return for a small gift of food, or perhaps a coin. There are many variations, but the words always follow a similar pattern and are not dissimilar to those used around Easter time.

Soul, soul for a souling cake
I pray you, missis, for a souling cake
Apple or pear, plum or cherry
Anything good to make us merry
Up with your kettles and down with your pans
Give us an answer and we'll be gone
Little Jack, Jack on his gate
Crying for butter to butter his cake
One for St Peter, two for St Paul
Three for the man that made us all.

Soul cakes are baked using currants and spices, with a cross marked on the top. They are similar to the Good Friday hot cross buns but in this case the cross, and cake, represents the memory of a soul who has died and is in purgatory.

The **Halton Souling Play** takes a similar form to the traditional mumming plays that are performed at Christmas time (see page 158) and the Kent hoodening traditions (see page 121). The script, which is based on one used in the 19th century, features the traditional cast of mummers, including St George and the Dragon, Beelzebub and the Quack Doctor.

Pumpkins and lanterns

Across the country, carved **pumpkins** can be seen on doorsteps at Hallowe'en, and there are many pumpkin carving events and competitions staged. The origins of this tradition probably come from legend, and the tale of **Jack-o'-lantern** or **Stingy Jack**.

In legend, Jack-o'-lantern is the name that it sometimes ascribed to the phosphorescent marsh gases that we also call Will-o'-the-wisp, which were said to lead people astray or sometimes show them a safe path through dangerous bogs and mires.

Jack-o'-lantern was known as a perennial trickster. So bad was he that when he died God did not want him in heaven and the Devil refused to have him in hell. Legend says that the Devil threw a hot coal at Jack to keep him away from the underworld and that Jack caught this in a turnip, which became the first turnip lantern. Jack was thus doomed to roam the earth for all time, neither in heaven nor in hell.

From this story come the pumpkins that people now carve as decorations; they are commonly known as Jack-o'-lanterns in America, although the term is used far less in Britain. It was more traditional in Britain and Ireland to carve turnips (or swedes) than it was pumpkins. Irish people who settled in

America made the switch to pumpkins and the vegetable was brought to Europe in the 17th century, where it began to take over from the customary turnips and other root vegetables. Pumpkins are much easier to carve.

How the legend of Jack-o'-lantern and the ascribing of the name to the carved vegetables arose is uncertain. Embers would traditionally be placed into turnips to ward off the spirit of Jack or other ghosts that were roaming abroad at this time of the year. We can see the symbolism of the skull-like design on the pumpkin (death) and the light (the fire of hell), and also the need to be able to light a path when people were out souling or house-visiting at this time. We can also see the parallel here with the religious beliefs of this time and the intercession for souls in purgatory. Jack was the first person in this state, caught in a liminal world.

Jack-o'-lantern was known as a perennial trickster.

Undoubtedly, very closely connected to all of this is the festival of **Punkie Night**, which can be seen in the Somerset village of Hinton St George on the last Thursday of October. The word Punkie, sometimes also spelt Punky, refers to a mangelwurzel – a member of the beetroot vegetable family grown predominantly as cattle feed – that has been hollowed out and a lighted candle put inside.

The children of the village carry lighted Punkie lanterns during the evening in a parade, visiting houses and reciting a rhyme for the occasion:

It's punkie night tonight
It's punkie night tonight
Give us a candle, give us a light
It's punkie night tonight.

Although very obviously linked to Samhain and house-visiting traditions, another legend has grown up around Punkie Night. The men of the village, it says, would go off to the fair at Chiselborough, some 4 miles distant, where they would drink so much that they would be unable to find their way back home. This prompted their wives to use the mangelwurzels as lanterns to find their errant husbands.

The main problem with this story, of course, is that it suggests the men would only go out drinking and find themselves in such a sorry state on just one night of the year. How likely does that seem?

Guy Fawkes Day (or Night)

Following on closely from Hallowe'en is **Guy Fawkes Day**, held in commemoration of the failed attempt to blow up the Houses of Parliament in 1605. Its alternative name, **Bonfire Night**, might also be seen to provide a bridge between the customs in memory of a historical event and the traditions of older fire festivals.

The date of 5 November became a national day of celebration as early as 1606, just one year after the Gunpowder Plot was foiled. Despite his name now being used to mark the event, the plan to blow up the Palace of Westminster was not led by Guy (or Guido) Fawkes, but by Robert Catesby. The group involved were Roman Catholics looking to re-establish Catholic rule in England by killing King James I, who had refused to allow more religious tolerance. The fact that Fawkes was the one captured in the cellar with the gunpowder the night before has made him the 'poster boy' for the festival.

One of the major components of a traditional Bonfire Night celebration is the fireworks display, symbolising the explosions that never took place. In this book we have seen a number of examples of how celebrations and customs can be shaped and are altered over time. This can happen through necessity, desire for change or sometimes when an old custom is revived.

It may be that, given increasing concerns over the environmental impact of fireworks and issues around animal welfare, not to mention the trauma that explosions can trigger for some army veterans, firework displays may not continue in their current form for very much longer. Recent developments in technology have provided the opportunity to explore other options, such as choreographed drone shows, set to music and painting a different kind of picture in the night sky. Discussions are already taking place in some areas, but as yet without firm decisions being made.

Another traditional element that has already all but disappeared from Bonfire Night festivals is the effigy of the

'Guy'. We have already seen how the ritual destruction of an effigy is central to many customs that centre around the land. In this case, the effigy was used to publicly condemn a hated figure, in a similar tradition to that of the Burning of the Bartle (see page 90).

In fact, in the Devon village of Chulmleigh, the Guy burned on 5 November was not symbolic of Guy Fawkes. Here in the 19th century it was customary for the young people of the parish to model their effigies on members of the community who had caused problems during the year, or who were disliked. These effigies would then be taken and burned in front of the house of the person who they were designed to represent.

Children making effigies and taking them through the streets, asking those they met for a **'penny for the Guy'**, was common in the 19th century, and for much of the 20th century too, before the custom began to die out. In the northern counties of Yorkshire and Lancashire there used to be a house-visiting tradition known as **Cob Coaling**, where groups would go from house to house and sing a traditional song for the occasion, in the hope that in return they would be given money for fireworks or materials for a bonfire.

There are definite parallels between this custom and souling that took place a few days before, as well as the wassailing traditions of the Christmas period, which blessed the apple trees for the coming year (see page 173). The Cob Coaling song borrows some lyrics from the traditional folk song 'Christmas is Coming' and probably also has roots in the songs used as part of mummers' performances (see page 158).

Torchlit processions and **burning barrels** used to be quite common on 5 November, and a few of these ceremonies still exist. Probably the most spectacular takes place at Ottery St Mary, in Devon. The usual practice for these customs was to set light to tar-coated barrels and to roll them through the streets; this still happens in nearby Hatherleigh as part of their carnival on the second Saturday of November.

At some point, one bright spark in Ottery St Mary decided that they could go one better, and so began the tradition of carrying burning tar barrels on one's shoulders instead. Ottery is the only place in the country where you can see this taking place. The spectacle draws large crowds, as you might expect for such a rare and dangerous activity, and it is now part of a wider weekend of events linked to the town's carnival. Events on the main day always begin at 5.30am with the firing of **rock cannons.**

These weapons are hand cannons fashioned from a length of bent metal pipe, with a percussive blasting cap mounted some 3 inches from one end. The short section at the end of the pipe is filled with rock powder, a type of gunpowder used for blasting and from which the cannons take their name, and is fired by striking the cap with a metal paddle. No projectile is used, but a loud noise is produced as the rock-powder ignites. At one time, as many as 30 of the local men would have owned a rock cannon, each one fashioned by the local blacksmith for the occasion.

Another custom featuring small cannon can be found at Fenny Stratford in Buckinghamshire. Each year on 11 November (or the day before if this is a Sunday) six small cannons in the shape of tankards are fired in a short ceremony. The firing of the **Fenny Poppers**, as they are known, is done in memory of Dr Thomas Willis, who died on this date, St Martin's Day, in 1675.

Thomas's grandson, Browne Willis, founded a new church, dedicated to St Martin, which was consecrated in May 1730 by the Bishop of Lincoln. It is said that Willis started the tradition of firing the small cast-iron mugs, packed with gunpowder and ignited with a long poker, in the middle of the 18th century, but this is difficult to confirm. The earliest written record appears to be from around 1830.

During the Second World War, the firing of the Fenny Poppers was halted due to noise abatement laws but they returned a few years later, although not without incident. In 1949, the blast from one of the cannons blew out a piece of the church clock's face, ironically just behind the large board erected in front of the tower on which the amount of money raised for church restoration was being recorded.

Turning the Devil's Stone

Not all customs fixed upon 5 November are related to fires and explosions. Returning to Devon, the small village of Shebbear is home to a custom that must take place on this date in order to ensure good fortune for the year ahead.

The apotropaic, or protective, ceremony that takes place in Shebbear is known as **Turning the Devil's Stone**. The stone in question lies on the village green and measures some 6 feet by 4 feet. Such stones in the landscape that appear out of place are usually glacial erratics that have been moved large distances on ice floes in the distant past and dumped in a new home; folklore has evolved to explain how they came to be where they are.

It would take the Devil a full year to make his way back to the surface and so, by turning the stone each November, he is reburied and kept safely out of the way where he cannot cause harm to the area.

The bell-ringers at Shebbear enter the church prior to the ceremony and ring a discordant peal of the bells, after which they make their way to the green. Here, observed by other residents of the village, they will use crowbars to upend and overturn the large stone; it will then remain in that position for the next 12 months until it is turned back again.

As you might guess from its name, the Devil's Stone was said to have been deposited in Shebbear by the Prince of Darkness himself, but there are also a number of alternative explanations.

Possibly, when the Devil was expelled from heaven St Michael dropped the stone on him, trapping him underneath. It would take the Devil a full year to make his way back to the surface and so, by turning the stone each November, he is reburied and kept safely out of the way where he cannot cause harm to the area.

In another story, the stone was intended for the building of the nearby church at Henscott. Each night the Devil would remove the stone and place it in Shebbear in an effort to stop the church being completed, until eventually it was just left there. This story is slightly less satisfying because it offers no explanation for why the stone needs to be turned.

One story that offers equally improbable explanation says the Devil placed the stone there to use as a chair and by turning it over each year the villagers are ensuring that he can never get too comfortable.

Much like the firing of the Fenny Poppers, the Turning of the Devil's Stone feels like an old tradition but is a more modern creation. *The Times* newspaper published an article in 1952 headlined 'Turning the Devil's Boulder, Primitive Rite in Village of Shebbear' in which it was suggested that the custom was a 'traditional survival'. In fact, there appear to be no written records prior to the 20th century, and the custom was probably a Victorian creation. Perhaps it is no coincidence that it takes place right outside the village pub, The Devil's Stone Inn.

Parish ceremonies

A short but nonetheless significant ceremony, which dates back many hundreds of years, takes place on 11 November on Knightlow Hill, which is not far from Ryton-on-Dunsmore in Warwickshire. Although not connected with one of the quarter days, which were the more usual time for paying rents and other dues, this tradition can be traced to a time when the commoners of the area would pay the local landowner for the right to drive cattle over their land.

The **Wroth Silver Ceremony** takes place at the remains of an old stone cross known as the Wroth Stone. The name of each local parish is called out and a representative from that parish comes forward and places the amount for which their parish is liable on the stone. In the modern version of the ceremony these are token amounts that total less than £1, but they still reference the original differences in value between each parish, based on their assessment at the time of the Domesday survey.

Every parish always pays their due at the Wroth Silver Ceremony, but at one time there were forfeits for any that didn't. Usually this was a levied fine to the value of £1 for each penny owing, but at some point an alternative punishment arose, which involved producing a white bull with red ears and a red nose.

It has been speculated that this change was probably made in the 18th century by the 2nd Duke of Montagu, who was fond of a joke. That being said, it is interesting to note that the image of a white cow, or bull, with red ears is a strong image in old folk and fairy tales. Numerous examples can be found; for instance, the **Morrigan** – the shapeshifting Celtic goddess of war and destiny – is described in the ancient Irish tale 'The Cualnge Cattle-Raid' as follows:

> *Thither then the Morrigan came in the shape of a white, hornless, red-eared heifer, with fifty heifers about her and a chain of silvered bronze between each two of the heifers.*

A custom is still observed in the Knowle area of Bristol on a Saturday in October each year that is likely to be even older than the Wroth Silver Ceremony. It has been suggested that the **St Mary Redcliffe Pipe Walk**, which is reminiscent of the Beating of the Bounds (see page 38), is the oldest custom of this type that can still be seen today.

In 1190 Robert de Berkeley, an Anglo-Saxon baron, donated water to the parish here by means of the installation of pipework. Originally the pipes were probably made of wood, before being replaced with lead and later with cast iron. A brass drinking fountain, which was installed in 1932, pays homage to this act with an inscription in Latin above a lion's head:

For the health and soul of Robert de Berkeley, who gave to God and the church of St Mary Redcliffe and its ministers the Rugewell and conduit. AD 1190.

The Pipe Walk takes place each year, following the original route of the conduit. It takes walkers through a number of private gardens but access is usually granted for the sake of tradition. The original purpose of the walk would have been to inspect the pipe for signs of damage and this is still done even though the water supply has long since been provided via more modern pipework. The Pipe Walk not only connects the participants with the area's past, but also helps to preserve the remaining elements of the original supply.

At various places along the route there are stone markers bearing the initials 'S.M.P.' These probably replaced earlier markers indicating the route. New walkers who take part in the custom today are ritually bumped against the stones as they are passed. This is reminiscent of the way that boys would be beaten, or have their heads bumped against stones, at each boundary marker when beating the bounds of the parish in order to ensure that the locations would not be forgotten (see page 38).

Walkers assemble at the church of St Barnabas in Knowle where refreshments are served in advance of the start of the walk at 10am. The party makes its way to the nearby wellhead that formed the source of the water, now located underneath a trapdoor in some nearby allotments. After the trap is opened, and the protective metal grille beneath is unlocked, everyone has an opportunity to observe the pipe. Then there is a short ceremony where the local vicar blesses the water and the party sets off for the 1½-mile perambulation to the pipe's end.

As the end of November approaches, we start to see the early signs of winter traditions, particularly the approaching Christmas festivities (apart from supermarkets, of course, who would like us to believe that Christmas starts in September!).

At the manor house of Cotehele in Cornwall, now looked after by the National Trust, volunteers spend many days assembling a garland 60 feet long, comprising 40,000 or more dried flowers. This hangs in the manor's hall right through the Christmas period.

Garlands and greenery, as we shall see, are as important to our midwinter customs and traditions as they are to those in the other four seasons.

Meteorological winter:
1 December to 28 February (29 in leap years)

Astronomical winter:
Winter solstice (near 22 December) to
vernal equinox (near 20 March)

Over the land freckled with snow half-thawed
The speculating rooks at their nests cawed
And saw from elm-tops, delicate as flowers of grass,
What we below could not see, Winter pass.

'Thaw' by Edward Thomas (1878–1917)

Winter

As we have seen time and again, the seasons and the weather were of the utmost importance to ancient peoples. In a similar vein to the more modern Wheel of the Year (see page 9), it is no surprise that the sun has been an ancient focus of worship and that so much of our seasonal folklore connects with it. Norse beliefs depicted the sun as a wheel, which changed the seasons as it moved. In their mythology, this wheel is called 'houl' which has led many to speculate that this is the derivation of the word 'yule'.

A great many of our annual customs are linked to times of celebration, of giving thanks or of welcome.

In many respects, there is probably a less diverse range of festivals taking place over the winter period than during the other seasons. This is perhaps unsurprising when a great many of our annual customs are linked to times of celebration, of giving thanks or of welcome. There are strong connections to the preparation of the land, the growth of crops and the hope for an abundant harvest.

Winter is a far more difficult time. The land is dormant, the weather is often harsh and communities are focussed on trying to make ends meet, surviving until the spring when life begins to return. Many customs observed during this season are grouped around Christmas and New Year, and then the pagan quarter-day festival of Imbolc in February.

Winter solstice and Yule

In modern times we now often conflate the terms Christmas and Yuletide, the latter being incorporated into the Christian celebrations. Yule is, of course, the old celebration related to the **winter solstice** – the date with the longest night of the year. The sun halts its decline for a few days at this point. This means that it rises in the same place each day, or appears to stand still in the sky.

In symbolic terms this can be seen as the **Festival of Rebirth**, because the sun needs to 'return' for the next year's cycle. In order to overcome the dark and drive away evil spirits, a ceremonial log was lit and burned at this time. This is the origin of the **Yule Log**, which is now a Christmas tradition. Another symbol of Christmas, **mistletoe**, has been attributed by many to the Druids. The plant was cut from oak trees, on which it often grew, and was given as a blessing. Mistletoe was a symbol of life, growing on the sacred tree – which would be leafless at this time of year.

Mistletoe was a symbol of life, growing on the sacred tree – which would be leafless at this time of year.

Evergreens are an important plant in winter as they symbolise eternal life. The bringing in of greenery for decoration has been carried forward to modern times, of course. Aside from mistletoe, we might see holly, whose spiky leaves offer protection against evil spirits; pine that represents healing and joy; and ivy that links to the idea of resurrection in the return of the sun. In Egyptian mythology, ivy is sacred to the god Osiris who rose from the dead; for the ancient Greeks, it is sacred to Dionysus, the god of vegetation and of returning spring.

The Christmas carol 'The Holly and the Ivy' seems to include these symbols of old nature-based religious practices alongside its Christian references, and therefore has a somewhat different character to many other traditional carols.

Solstice celebrations

Festivities marking the winter solstice are a real mix of old and new. As with the longest day in the summer, large numbers of people travel to Stonehenge in Wiltshire to mark the occasion, with the monument accessible for dawn celebrations. In Cornwall, much like the Golowan Midsummer festival (see page 62), a new interpretation of a traditional Cornish midwinter festival now takes place.

This event is called **Montol**; it refers to the winter solstice in the Cornish language and is an amalgamation of different aspects of some ancient Cornish practices described in written records. A large part of this celebration is a procession of musicians and dancers who are masked and costumed. This 'guising' might be seen as a derivative of the traditional mummers who perform their plays at this season (see page 158). The procession also features decorated paper lanterns, which are seen in other midwinter events.

The **Burning the Clocks** festival in the East Sussex town of Brighton is a community event involving a spectacular procession and bonfire. Members of the local community make paper lanterns constructed around willow frames, often following a different theme each year. After these have been carried through town in a procession, they are taken to the beach where a large bonfire is burning and are thrown into the flames to be consumed. This can be seen as a ritual offering to mark the end of the year and to express the hope that the next will be as good or better. The festival was created in the 1990s to celebrate the winter solstice and as a rejection of the over-commercialisation of Christmas.

Mummers' plays

Mummers' plays, to which winter solstice guising might be seen to have some parallels, have a long history and are commonly performed over the Yule period. They are short, dramatic pieces, with rhyming text and a cast of characters who might be familiar to their audiences.

There are three different types of mummers' play, the most frequently performed having the theme of **'hero and combat'**. These are commonly seen as part of Yuletide festivities. After a prologue, there are usually a number of challenges acted out that culminate in a sword fight between the hero and the villain. One of the two is slain, before the entrance of a quack doctor who effects a miraculous cure. The importance of this scene, and its links to rebirth and renewal, is obvious.

For this reason, as with so many of our customs, the view in the past was that the mummers' play was a folk practice that emerged from pre-Christian fertility rites. But the absence of written records on the matter between the distant past and the 19th century means that we do not have the evidence to be able to establish this for certain.

Although they are often conflated or confused, the mummers' play is quite distinct from medieval mystery plays, which are performed at Chester (see page 88), with their tableaux and tellings of biblical tales in song. The word 'mummer' most likely derives from the Germanic *mummenschanz* or *vermummen*, which refers to the act of wrapping or disguising your face. We can see the link here with the midwinter and Yule guising traditions, such as those seen at Montol.

We know that the mummer as a performer existed in the 13th century, because they are mentioned at the marriage of the daughter of King Edward I, which took place at Christmas. We do not know, however, the form this performance would have taken. The earliest existing text for a play similar to the ones we have now comes from an 18th-century chapbook – a small printed booklet.

After a prologue, there are usually a number of challenges acted out that culminate in a sword fight between the hero and the villain.

While the texts of early plays are still known today, these are a different form of folk play to the mumming types. It is during the height of the publication of chapbooks in the mid-1800s that we find many mummers' plays recorded, such as one entitled 'The Peace Egg', which relates to the Pace Egging traditions of Easter time (see page 19).

Another common type of mumming tradition is the **Sword Dance play**, where the folk dance dominates the drama. Often the acting and dancing elements are now split, with teams of sword dancers performing a separate mummers' play; performances of these tend to take place on 26 December, Boxing Day (see page 165).

Christmas

It has become increasingly difficult to separate the traditional elements of the modern Christmas from older Yule celebrations. Despite the views of today's retailers, Christmas Eve was the marker for the start of festivities, with the Yule log being placed on the fire, lit with the retained ashes of the previous year's log and burned for a 12-day period.

Hobby horses

Hobby horses are quite common over the Christmas period. As mentioned previously (see page 37), in East Kent there is the **Hooden Horse**, a man concealed by sacking and carrying a carved wooden horse's head on a pole, who performs with attendants. In the 19th century, they would tour local establishments, particularly on Christmas Eve, and expect payment for their appearance.

In one pub in West Sussex you might stand a chance of running into a live one on Christmas Day. The Fox Inn at Bucks Green was once two separate buildings, one of which was an almshouse, but at some point the two were joined together to become a single building. This involved enclosing a bridleway that used to run between the two.

In order to preserve an ancient law that states that driving livestock along such a path on an annual basis will maintain it as a right of way, a horse is now ridden along the bridleway every

Christmas Day, including through the pub, although it is usually led along this section rather than ridden. The custom is very popular locally and many villagers turn out to watch the horse's arrival around noon.

Probably the most striking and well known of the hobby horse folk customs over the Christmas period is the **Mari Lwyd**, which is generally associated with South Wales. The hobby here is again similar to the hooden horse, but is made from an actual horse's skull set on a pole, with a hinged jaw allowing it to snap. The pole is often covered with a white sheet to conceal the carrier, rather than the sackcloth often found with hooden horses.

The first written records of the custom date from the early 19th century, although these do state that it was already known as a tradition at this time. As with many customs, it fell out of favour in the early 1900s, but in recent decades it has been revived widely across Wales in its original form.

The Mari Lwyd is a house-visiting tradition that involves a party of horse and leader, with other costumed characters, visiting people's homes and trying to gain entry with the help of songs and rhymes. It was up to the occupants of the house to reply in a similar manner in an effort to stop the would-be visitors. Songs were often improvised, a little like a folkloric rap battle, and if the householders can't compete or give up, then the party enters the house and must be served food and drink, before moving on to the next location. There are clear parallels with other house-visiting traditions during the year.

Church bells

Many churches hold special services at midnight to celebrate the arrival of Christmas and the ringing of church bells on Christmas morning is a common sound. But in the West Yorkshire town of Dewsbury this is slightly different.

The bell peal at the church of Dewsbury Minster takes place each Christmas Eve, starting at around 10pm, and is known as **Tolling the Devil's Knell**. The custom is unique to this church.

A single bell, the tenor bell, is tolled once for each year since the birth of Christ, with the final toll taking place at midnight, thanks to a handy electronic counter that ensures the right number of years have been counted.

The bell is named **Black Tom** after Sir Thomas de Soothill, a local knight who, according to legend, drowned one of his servants in the mill pond as punishment for not having attended a Sunday church service. As penance, Sir Thomas installed the bell and perhaps the custom began from that time.

The bell is named Black Tom after Sir Thomas de Soothill, who, according to legend, drowned his servant in the mill pond.

Gift giving

Christmas is, as we know, a time of gift giving. As well as our own family and friends, it was a time when small gifts were also given to tradesfolk and domestic staff. These became known as **'Christmas boxes'**, which provides us with a possible explanation for the term Boxing Day (see page 165). Today we can still see some vestiges of these old customs in the form of charitable giving to the poor.

On Christmas Day at Sherborne Castle, in the county of Dorset, the Digby family who have been resident for many hundreds of years still maintain an ancient dole-giving custom. Traditionally, feudal doles at Christmas would be food or small amounts of money given to the poor of the parish, in recognition of what is a particularly difficult time of the year. Now, the family give out newly minted coins to anyone who turns up at the Estate Yard. The custom is known as the **Penny Dole** as this was the value of coin that used to be given out. Nowadays, recipients are either given a £1 or 50p coin, which is mounted on a small card with a Christmas greeting. They also receive a chocolate coin – because who doesn't need more chocolate at Christmas?

> *Traditionally, feudal doles at Christmas would be food or small amounts of money given to the poor of the parish.*

For a healthier treat on Christmas Day you could try Ripon Cathedral in North Yorkshire. The dole here probably has its origins in the medieval times and, today, sees apples distributed among the congregants by members of the choir. At one time, the fruits would have been adorned with rosemary, in memory of the Virgin Mary, but now they are handed out *au naturel*.

Twelve days of Christmas

Everyone is familiar with the Twelve Days of Christmas, but most people merely associate them with the song and the gifts that an unnamed, but extremely generous, 'true love' offers to their intended without any kind of consideration given to the storage of the 364 gifts, including 42 swans. Presumably the lucky recipient would need to enlist the services of a swan upping team (see page 96).

The festive period of 12 days refers to the time it took the Magi, often referred to as the three kings, to reach Bethlehem to visit the infant Christ. Historically, this was a holiday period that virtually everyone observed as it was a time of the year where no agricultural activity was taking place. Immediately after the end of this holiday, everyone would return to work and preparations would begin for the coming of spring.

Many of our customs and festivities at this time still link to the celebrations that took place in the Middle Ages. These would have begun with church services for the First Day (Christmas Day), much as we have midnight masses and other services today. The Second Day, the Feast of St Stephen or Boxing Day, still prompts the giving of alms to the poor.

Boxing Day

There are competing theories relating to the origins of the name Boxing Day as the second day of Christmastide but it may refer to the tradition of giving to those in need at this time and the placing of alms boxes in churches. At Greatham in County Durham, the almshouses now known as Greatham Hospital provide the backdrop for an annual performance of longsword dancing by the **Redcar Sword Dancers**.

The dancers wear military-style uniforms – a style of dress which is not unusual. The **Handsworth Traditional Sword**

Dancers in South Yorkshire dress in a similar fashion. The swords in these traditions have a handle on each end, with teams of up to eight performing a series of complex moves that lock the blades together in different patterns, usually ending with a star that is held in the air by the 'Captain'.

The Handsworth dancers also perform a mummers' play, a traditional one with local origins being the **Derby Tup**. The word 'tup' refers to the ram, which is put among the ewes for mating, although in the play **Old Tup** is more reminiscent of a horse than a ram. The hobby horse here is not unlike the Kentish hooden horse (see page 160) in its construction, although it does sport a pair of ram's horns. Although generally now performed in public places, the Derby Tup play would have historically been a house-visiting custom over the Christmas period.

Another story says that the bird betrayed St Stephen, who was hiding in a bush; the wren flapped its wings and alerted the saint's enemies as to his whereabouts.

In Ireland, another name for Boxing Day is **Wren Day**. There are several house-visiting customs relating to Christmas and, on 26 December, **Wrenboys** – both men and boys – dress in greenery, or traditional costume, and sing and play in return for a coin or a gift of food. Their name comes from the tradition of hunting a wren that would be placed on the top of a decorated pole, which formed part of the parade. Nowadays, where Wren Day observance still takes place, either a stuffed bird or more commonly a toy wren is used instead.

At the end of the parade, the wren would be buried along with one of the pennies collected, suggesting a ritual offering as we have seen in so many other practices.

It is not certain why the wren features in this particular custom. A couple of different explanations suggest that it is because of the treachery of the bird that it is hunted. In one of these stories, Irish forces were mounting a secret offensive against Cromwell's troops, but a wren stood on one of the drums and woke the English soldiers just in time to fend off the attack. Another story says that the bird betrayed St Stephen, who was hiding in a bush; the wren flapped its wings and alerted the saint's enemies as to his whereabouts.

There are a couple of other interpretations. One is rooted in the subsuming of older beliefs into newer ones as, according to medieval texts, the Irish word for 'wren' comes from the word *drean*, which means 'druid bird'. But as we have learned elsewhere, we need to be wary of these sorts of associations where there is little written evidence to back them up.

Another suggestion is that the legend relates to **Clíona** or **Clíodnha**, variously a sea goddess, **Queen of the Banshees** or a figure of the underworld. She would entice men to the ocean before drowning them. When a way of destroying her was discovered, she is said to have escaped by turning into a wren. The punishment for her crimes was to be forced to transform into a wren every Christmas Day and to die by human hands.

WHEN TO CUT
YOUR FINGERNAILS

Holy Innocents Day (28 December) is considered
to be the most unlucky day in the Christian year. The
date marks the slaughter of innocent children by King
Herod in an effort to kill Jesus. Traditionally, many tasks
were avoided on this day, including fishing and washing
clothes. Superstitious belief also says that you should
avoid cutting your nails on this day. However, to help
you to decide when it would be the best time for nail
trimming, an old rhyme gives some guidance:

Cut nails on a Monday, cut them for health
Cut them on a Tuesday, cut them for wealth
Cut them on Wednesday, cut them for news
Cut them on Thursday, a pair of new shoes
Cut them on Friday, cut them for sorrow
Cut them on Saturday, see your true love tomorrow
But cut them on Sunday, your safety seek
For Old Nick'll have you, the rest of the week

The positioning of the calcium flecks that are often
visible on nails were also used for divination; good
luck could be expected if the marks were
white, but blue was not so positive.

Molly dancers

A folk song called 'Cutty Wren' ('cutty' being northern dialect for 'small' or 'short') is often sung on St Stephen's Day and in the East Suffolk village of Middleton since the 1990s there has been a revival of an ancient custom called the **Cutty Wren Ceremony**, which is similar to the wrenboy traditions (see page 166). The custom now is performed on Boxing Day by the **Old Glory Molly Dancers** who lead a silent parade by torchlight, headed by a carved wren on top of a decorated staff. The procession moves from the village hall to the Bell Inn, where there are displays of Molly Dancing followed by songs and stories about the wren.

Molly Dancing was a midwinter morris dance tradition, which was performed in the main by ploughboys who were not able to find employment until the beginning of the planting season.

Molly Dancing was a midwinter morris dance tradition, which was performed in the main by ploughboys who were not able to find employment until the beginning of the planting season. As a tradition, Molly has been overlooked by most collectors of folk song and dance; sadly, it is likely that many of the original dances have now been lost.

It is commonly associated with Plough Monday (see page 187). Ploughboys would travel around their local area seeking to raise money through performance until they could work in the fields again.

Anyone who didn't pay the dancers was likely to wake up the following morning with a neatly ploughed furrow across their land. Guising (see page 157) was an important part of the tradition, as nobody would want to employ a ploughboy who had vandalised their land, so dancers would often use soot to blacken their faces and dress in their 'Sunday best' rather than their working clothes.

The straw bear costume is ritually burned – an offering to the land in anticipation of the first ploughing and planting of the coming spring.

The largest assembly of molly dancers can now to be found at Whittlesey in Cambridge as part of the **Straw Bear Festival**, which takes place over a January weekend. A man wearing an enormous and very heavy straw costume is led through the town on the Saturday, with many teams of molly and morris dancers following behind. Another important part of this procession is an old plough, pulled by 'ploughboys'. On the Sunday of Straw Bear weekend, after more performances from the dancers, the bear costume is ritually burned – an offering to the land in anticipation of the first ploughing and planting of the coming spring.

Sporting traditions

If you want to work off the excess Christmas food, there are many sporting traditions that take place around this time, often on Boxing Day. They have histories of varying lengths and nowadays tend to be staged as fundraisers for local charities.

Tug-of-war competitions, raft races and pram races are common. Also popular are football matches, which were often held between competing trades or other local services, such as the **Fishermen and Firemen match** in Scarborough, North Yorkshire, and the now defunct **Waltham Cross Bakers and Sweeps match** in Hertfordshire.

Kirkwall in Orkney still has a traditional **Ba' game** that takes place on both Christmas Day and New Year's Day (or the day after if either of these is a Sunday). Ba' here means 'ball' and Scottish Ba' games are a survival from medieval football, although at Kirkwall the game has developed into a version of handball – with very few rules.

The two competing teams in Kirkwall are known as the **Uppies** and **Doonies**, which refers to the two opposite ends of the town. Each team has a goal where they must try to place the ball. For the Uppies, the ball needs to hit the end of a house opposite the Catholic church. For their opponents, the ball needs to end up in the water of the harbour. The winning side will elect one player as 'victor', usually someone who has taken part and performed well for many years. They are awarded the ball as a trophy, which they get to keep.

Wassailing

Traditionally the Third Day of Christmas, the Feast of St John on 27 December, featured a lot of wine. The story of John's life tells how the saint was offered a glass of poisoned wine while he was visiting the ancient city of Ephesus. He survived this attempt on his life because he blessed the wine before he drank it, at which point the poison slid out of the cup in the form of a small green snake. Christian art often shows this scene.

Historically, people of all classes would drink toasts at feasts on this day, passing around a wassail bowl. The term 'wassail' is thought to come from the Anglo Saxon words *waes* and *hael*, being a toast to good health. Some suggest the root as the Norse for 'be healthy', *ves heill*, and in both cases the meaning is the same.

The custom of **wassailing** now takes place on various dates during January and the ritual is intended to encourage a good harvest from the cider orchards in

Saucepans will be beaten, and cries go up from the assembled crowds.

the forthcoming year. At a commonly occurring ceremony, toast is soaked in cider made from the previous year's crop and then tied to a branch of an apple tree. Saucepans and other metal containers will be beaten, and shouts and cries go up from the assembled crowds; the purpose of the cacophony is to drive away evil spirits from the trees. In years gone by, farmers may also have fired their shotguns into the air.

Prayers may be offered up to the trees in the form of traditional recited verse; there are a number of variations, but all contain similar phrases.

Old Apple Tree, Old Apple Tree,
We wassail thee and hope that thou wilt bear;
For the Lord doth know where we shall be
Till apples come another year.
For to bear well and to bloom well,
So merry let us be;
Let every man take off his hat and shout to thee,
Old Apple Tree, Old Apple Tree,
We wassail thee and hope that thou wilt bear
Hat fulls,
Cap fulls,
Three bushel bag fulls,
And a little heap under the stairs.

Many orchards in Britain still hold wassail celebrations today, recreating the original form. If you don't live in the countryside, this doesn't preclude you from finding a wassail, as there are a growing number of **urban wassails** taking place. In the London Borough of Hackney, for example, wassails are held in small community orchards.

In Tarring Village, Worthing, the wassail takes the form of a torchlit procession in the main street ending up at the Vine Pub, where the ceremony occurs in the beer garden, next to a single apple tree. Over the last few years in Willesden Green, London, urban wassails have been held outside the area's independent shops to give thanks for them and to wish them success in the coming year. This new adaptation of an old tradition brings the whole community together in a positive way.

In areas of the country where fruit was not grown, wassailing took a slightly different form, and was another house-visiting tradition. Groups of people would go door to door, carrying a wassail bowl with which to drink people's health and singing traditional songs.

The Christian tradition of singing Christmas carols, perhaps in return for a small donation to church funds or a local charity, owes much to these wassails. In fact, the popular Christmas carol 'We Wish You a Merry Christmas' contains direct references to old wassailing songs. House-visiting wassails began in some places to become synonymous with drunken behaviour and demands for gifts, leading to trouble if they were not forthcoming – much like trick or treating at Hallowe'en. The line 'So bring us some figgy pudding' followed by the threat 'We won't go until we've got some', hints at such bad behaviour in the past.

In the Cornish town of Bodmin, the house-visiting continues, with a group of wassailers dressed in fine suits and top hats. Written records of the tradition here can be found as far back as the 17th century when the town clerk donated a wassail bowl to the community. At this time, wassailing took place at the mayor's residence; to commemorate this, the town council offices form a starting point for a tour of venues that takes up to 12 hours to complete.

New Year

The Seventh and Eighth Days of Christmas – New Year's Eve and New Year's Day – give rise to customs and celebrations that close the old year and bring in the new, as happens at other times of year for different reasons.

Fire is a popular theme and may be seen as ceremonially destroying the spirits of winter, preparing the way for the spring gods, and as a time of birth and renewal. While fire ceremonies can be found all over Britain, they are especially common in the north.

The fire custom that is celebrated in the market place at Allendale, Northumberland, at midnight on 31 December is like a sedate form of the Running of the Tar Barrels at Ottery St Mary (see page 145). In Allendale, the **Tar Bar'ls** are cut in half to form a sort of trough, which is filled with tar and lit. These are carried by a procession of people in fancy dress, which is a common part of New Year celebrations but also harks back to guising traditions. At the end of the walk the barrels are used to light the main bonfire, where the assembled crowds sing the traditional New Year's Eve anthem of 'Auld Lang Syne'.

> *Fire is a popular theme of these customs and may be seen as ceremonially destroying the spirits of winter.*

NEW YEAR
LOVE DIVINATION

An old ritual from the Peak District brings a whole
new meaning to the term 'Ringing in the New Year'.
It was traditional to make a drink known as a 'posset'
on 31 December, to serve at the final party of the old
year. A posset was a drink made with a milk base.
This would be curdled with either beer or wine,
and other ingredients – including eggs, spices
and currants – would then be added.

Possets were usually heated for drinking and
were often used as a curative. For this particular ritual,
however, the posset was served cold. When the jug was
placed on the table, the matriarch of the household
would drop her wedding ring into the liquid. After a
good stirring, everyone would ladle a serving of the
posset for themselves into a mug. Whoever got the ring
would be likely to wed in the New Year.

Hogmanay

Hogmanay is the Scottish celebration of New Year's Eve. While the Tar Bar'ls is happening south of the border, in Perthshire another fire-based cleansing ritual takes place. The **Flambeaux Procession** at Comrie on Tayside sees a number of 3-metre poles topped with flaming sackcloth being carried through the streets. Again, members of the procession wear fancy dress but this time, at the end of the parade, the torches are ceremonially cast into the River Earn as a form of offering.

Probably the most impressive and memorable of all the Scottish fire festivals is **Up Helly Aa** in Lerwick in the Shetland Isles. In fact, there are 12 Up Helly Aas that take place between January and March, but this is the largest. Inspired by the area's past, the festival culminates with the burning of a Viking longship.

Before this, there are performances of traditional music from the islands, along with guising and a torch procession. At one time, as in other places, burning barrels would be rolled through the streets, but this stopped in 1874.

If you are looking for the ultimate in dangerous fire displays, then you should probably see in the New Year at Stonehaven in Aberdeenshire. As the clock strikes midnight a procession wends its way up the High Street, consisting of people twirling flaming wooden balls on wires or chains that have been covered in fabric and soaked in paraffin, before being lit. Imagine if a shot putter from the Highland Games had had too much of the celebratory whisky and decided to step things up a notch! At the end of the night, the balls are all thrown into the sea in the same manner as the Flambeaux poles in Comrie.

One of the Scottish fire festivals has ignored the calendar change and has stubbornly kept to 11 January, the original New Year's Day. This is the **Burning of the Clavie** that takes place in Burghead in Moray; it is a particularly long-standing tradition, having reportedly changed little over many hundreds of years. It is an ancient tradition that provides a more personal token of protection for the coming year, rather than an offering to the land.

A clavie is a half-barrel, not unlike those at Allendale (see page 176). Originally, herring barrels would have been used as there was a thriving fishing industry in the area. In the modern ceremony, whisky barrels held together with iron hoops stand in for the herring barrels. These are nailed onto a post, which is used to carry them, with the custom dictating that the same nail is used each year.

Once set alight, a succession of local men carry the clavie through the streets, sometimes stopping at the houses formerly occupied by town dignitaries; the modern residents are presented with embers from the barrel as a symbol of good luck. These were traditionally used to light New Year fires in their homes. Eventually, the clavie reaches the site of an old altar at the fort on Doorie Hill, where it is placed on the ground and more fuel is added. The mass burns down to a pile of ash and cinders, and during this time onlookers pull burning pieces of wood from the fire, which they take home for good luck. Some people even send cold embers to those who no longer live in the area, and many people nail the wood over their door, much as you would a horseshoe, to act as a symbol of good luck and protection.

While Hogmanay is similar to the bringing in of the New Year in other parts of Britain, Scotland's celebrations tend to last for three or four days and include some extra elements. **First Footing** customs, for example, occur more widely in Scotland and with a greater sense of importance. Many people head home to observe the ritual at the end of the fire celebrations.

First Footing relates to the first person to enter your house on

New Year's Day. What they look like, and what gifts they bring, is said to invite either good or bad luck for the next 12 months. In many areas a dark-haired man is said to bring good luck; it has been suggested that this may allude to the past incursions of Norse invaders, who would generally be fair haired. While this is certainly possible, there are regional variations in both the preferred hair colour and gender of the first footer.

Aside from the first footer's physical appearance, the gifts that they bring are also important. A coin is usual, representing good

fortune; shortbread to symbolise an abundance of food, and a lump of coal for warmth. In Scotland, naturally, a glass of whisky is essential for good health

Epiphany

The final important celebration of the Christmas period comes on the Twelfth Day, 6 January, known in the Christian calendar as Epiphany. In the Bible story, this is when the Magi arrived in Bethlehem to present their gifts to the infant Jesus.

Countrywide, there are particular traditions associated with the end of Christmas. This is the date, for example, after which it is considered to be bad luck to still have your greenery (or Christmas decorations) up in the house. Seventeenth-century poet Robert Herrick addressed the topic of taking down your Christmas greenery in 'Ceremony Upon Candlemas Eve' with a stark warning:

Down with the rosemary, and so
Down with the bays and mistletoe;
Down with the holly, ivy, all
Wherewith ye dress'd the Christmas hall;
That so the superstitious find
No one least branch there left behind;
For look, how many leaves there be
Neglected there, maids, trust to me,
So many goblins you shall see.

There are also numerous regional customs marking this time. In the fields of North Lincolnshire, the **Haxey Hood Game** is contested each year on 6 January (or the day before if this falls on a Sunday). The game dates from the 14th century, and four pubs from the villages of Haxey and Westwoodside put forward teams to compete.

The 'hoods' take the form of a leather tube that each of the teams must try to return to their pub and present to the landlord or

> *Teams carry the hood by forming massive scrums of people, called 'sways'.*

landlady, who will then keep it until the next year's game. Teams carry the hood by forming massive scrums of people, called 'sways'. These can become so big that during one game, in 2002, a sway swept up a parked car and moved it 10 feet along the road. Since this time, roads are kept clear on the day of the game.

In charge of the game is the **Lord of the Hood**, assisted by a number of referees, called **boggins**, who uphold the few rules that apply. One final character is a traditional **Fool**, dressed in rags, who leads a procession to the fields before the game commences. Before the start of the Haxey Hood, the Fool declares:

House against house
Town against town
If a man meets a man
Knock him down, but don't hurt him.

After the speech, a ritual known as **'Smoking the Fool'** takes place. In the modern version of the game a fire is lit behind the Fool and the smoke wafts over him. In the traditional version, the Fool would have been suspended over the fire until he began to choke, before being cut down and having the opportunity to escape. This could be regarded as a similar form of the protective smoke from fires lit at Samhain (see page 134).

The Haxey Hood Game is said to derive from an occasion in the year 1359, when the wife of a local landowner, Lady de Mowbray, was riding between the two competing villages when she lost her silk riding hood in a gust of wind. A group of men who were working in the field nearby rushed to pick it up for her. The man who got there first was very shy and could not bring himself to return the item, so he passed it to another man to do it instead.

One final character is a traditional Fool, dressed in rags, who leads a procession to the fields.

Lady de Mowbray, it is said, declared the man who returned the hood a lord in his behaviour, but the other man was a fool for not wanting to approach her, and we see these two characters reflected in the game today. She donated 13 acres of land with the covenant that a game should be played on them each year in memory of the event.

It is common, of course, in folklore for such stories to grow up around very old traditions such as the Haxey Hood Game. There is no written record of Lady de Mowbray's bequest, but we certainly cannot dismiss it. There was a landowner at the time named de Mowbray, and what is reported to have happened to Lady de Mowbray is not especially unusual or notable, so maybe it did.

St Distaff's Day

With the decorations put away and the festive food and drink consumed, people would return to work on 7 January. The men would soon be preparing for the start of the agricultural season, while the women would take up their household work, such as spinning. From the 12th century until the Industrial Revolution, most women would spin using a distaff and spindle, rather than the more expensive and cumbersome spinning wheel, and 7 January is often known now as **St Distaff's Day**.

Women would spin using a distaff and spindle, rather than the more expensive and cumbersome spinning wheel.

What is unusual about this is that there is no Catholic saint named Distaff. Also known as **Distaff Day**, or sometimes **Rock Day**, it is unclear when the prefix 'saint' was added. It probably came about in imitation of the naming of Catholic feast days throughout the year.

It appears that the transition from holiday time to work used to be taken a little less seriously than it is now. As the women returned to their spinning, the men – perhaps wanting to prolong the holiday spirit – would try to set fire to their flax. To try and stop this, save the flax and put the men off, the women would throw buckets of water at them.

Robert Herrick also penned a verse about St Distaff's Day, which appears in his *Hesperides* (1648):

Partly work and partly play
You must on St Distaff's Day:
From the plough soon free your team;
Then come home and fother them;
If the maids a-spinning go,
Burn the flax and fire the tow.
Bring in pails of water then,
Let the maids bewash the men.
Give St Distaff all the right:
Then bid Christmas sport good night,
And next morrow every one
To his own vocation.

Herrick seems to be showing here that the day is something of a transition period, with normal hard work definitely resuming the day after. It is also interesting to note that when Herrick is writing in the 17th century, the word 'saint' already seems to have come into use.

Once the menfolk finally get back to work, then thoughts will soon be turning to preparing the land for the return of growth in the spring.

Plough Monday

In terms of the ritual year, we can see the approach of the new agricultural year represented in two significant ways: one associated with the old pagan ways and the other with Christian festivals. As we've seen, there is still some crossover between these two.

The first Monday following Epiphany is known as **Plough Monday** and is now regarded as the marker for the start of the agricultural year, with the term coming into use during the 15th century. On the day before, **Plough Sunday**, it is still common in many places to see church services taking place to bless the plough before work commences. In fact, it is usually not the plough itself that is taken into the church, but rather a ploughshare. This is the part of the plough which consists of a board or frame with the cutting blades mounted on it.

It is still common in many places to see church services taking place to bless the plough before work commences.

Although more often found in rural churches, where agricultural work remains a staple of the local economy, Plough Sunday services still take place in larger places of worship, such as the cathedrals in Exeter and Durham. The services are often preceded by a procession that contains ancient traditional elements. In Durham, for example, ribbons are attached to the plough as a sign of luck, much like those tied to clootie trees (see page 67), and the implement is drawn through the streets to the cathedral for the service. It is accompanied by a number of costumed attendants, with sword and morris dancing also taking place.

This procession recalls what would have been traditional practices on Plough Monday, which are very recognisable from other seasonal customs. The plough would have been taken round during house-visiting as a means of collecting doles. Musicians would often play and a Fool was often present.

Dancers use a repertoire of six dances, accompanied by musicians and helped, or hindered, by the Fool.

In North Yorkshire, we can see these characters as part of the **Goathland Plough Stots**, a traditional longsword dance team that performs each year, usually on the Saturday following Plough Monday. Dancers use a repertoire of six dances, accompanied by musicians and helped, or hindered, by the Fool. The word 'stot' is one of a number of names for those who would have worked alongside the plough. Aside from **Stots** and **Ploughboys**, there were also **Jacks** – a common name in folklore, as we have already seen with the Jack in the Green customs (see page 124), **Bullocks** and, more unusually, **Witches**.

In a similar tradition to the mummers' hero-and-combat play, **Plough plays** used to be performed around Plough Monday, but these were confined to the East Midlands and East Anglia. These plays were also known as **Wooing plays** and always followed a similar plot line. A young man tries to win the hand of a lady but she rejects him and instead chooses the Fool. Despondent, he joins the army at the request of a Recruiting Sergeant. Another female character arrives and accuses the Fool of fathering her illegitimate baby; after this, the play reverts to the usual hero-and-combat format, along with a death and revival scene with the doctor, reflecting the rebirth of the land after winter.

A young man tries to win the hand of a lady but she rejects him and chooses the Fool.

A number of revivals of Plough plays can now be seen in the same areas where they were originally performed. These include the Nottinghamshire towns of Newark-on-Trent and Calverton, where they are enacted by the beautifully named Calverton Real Ale and Plough Play Society – or CRAPPS for short.

Needle and Thread Gaudy

Not all long-running traditions are as public or as well known as some of those we have seen so far. Such is the case at Oxford University where a private celebration takes place at Old New Year, on 11 January, involving some members of Queen's College. This ceremony is known as the **Needle and Thread Gaudy**.

The term 'gaudy' refers here to a particular type of celebratory dinner that is held in some older colleges or private schools in Britain. The name comes from the Latin, meaning 'to rejoice'.

The Needle and Thread Gaudy is a private ceremony with attendance by invitation only, and is usually open to graduates who joined the college in a particular year – known as matriculation year – alongside current students at the college. At the meal, the college bursar (who is responsible for finances) presents each attendee with a needle and length of thread, telling them to 'take this and be thrifty'. Providing each guest with the means of mending the hoods of their academic gowns was a symbolic reminder not to squander their money.

At the meal, the college bursar (who is responsible for finances) presents each attendee with a needle and length of thread, telling them to 'take this and be thrifty'.

The ceremony derives from a gentle jibe at Robert de Eglesfield, chaplain of Queen Philippa of Hainault, who founded the college in 1341 and named it in her honour. The name of the custom is a play on words: the French word *aiguille* meaning 'needle' and *fil* meaning 'thread' form an approximation of the chaplain's surname when spoken together, as well as being a gentle reminder of the need for simple living.

Imbolc

Before the modern calendar and Christian festivals, the coming of spring was marked midway between the winter solstice and vernal (spring) equinox with the celebration that we now call **Imbolc**. Pronounced 'im'olk', this is a traditional Gaelic festival

that is now conflated with the feast day of St Brigid, one of the patron saints of Ireland.

As with other ancient festivals, it is impossible to know how they would have been celebrated originally and how they have evolved into what we know now. It seems likely that St Brigid is intrinsically linked with the Gaelic goddess Brigid, who was – among her many attributes – associated with fertility. In mythology, Brigid was pregnant with the seed of the sun, symbolic of seeds germinating and growing in the soil.

It is traditional at Imbolc to make Brigid's Crosses, which are woven out of rushes or straw. The crosses are made up of a central square with four arms set at right angles.

It is traditional at Imbolc to make **Brigid's Crosses**, which are woven out of rushes or straw. Many people in Ireland still follow this practice today. The crosses are made up of a central square with four arms set at right angles. They are often hung in the kitchen as protection against evil and fire.

Fire was an important part of ritual Imbolc celebrations, as with all the equinox and quarter day festivals. Today, Imbolc is a mix of revived customs, adapted by neopagan groups who follow their own rituals with many traditional elements included, as well as, in some cases, creative new performances.

A popular example of these new developments is the **Imbolc Fire Festival** held at Marsden, West Yorkshire, which began in the 1990s and has grown into a significant community event where you can find many traditional elements of old festivities. At first, the Marsden Fire Festival began with a small number of entertainers, including fire eaters and dancers, but now it includes people carrying torches and wearing masks depicting animals, the sun and the moon.

Central to the Marsden festival is a symbolic battle between the **Green Man** and the character of **Jack Frost**. Both are giants, standing head and shoulders above anyone else in the procession. The two face off, while their attendants twirl fire torches, acting out the conflict between the two. Eventually, the character of Jack Frost turns away defeated; the Green Man is victorious in driving out winter and spring arrives. The event concludes with fireworks, making the whole festival a spectacular performance of music, fire and drama.

At St Blazey in Cornwall, a lantern parade and church service connected with Imbolc takes place on 3 February. The **St Blaise Feast** celebrates St Blaise, the patron saint of the area's wool industry, but also, curiously, of sore throats. Again, the festival is a revival that joins together the saint's day and Imbolc. In honour of the saint's associations, the church service includes an unusual element called the **Blessing of the Throats**, where

> *Central to the Marsden festival is a symbolic battle between the Green Man and the character of Jack Frost. Both are giants, standing head and shoulders above anyone else in the procession.*

the vicar and the local bishop hold crossed candles up to the throat of each person in attendance and say a special prayer.

The Blessing of the Throats is not unique to St Blazey, however, and other examples are found around Britain, the most well known probably being at the Church of St Etheldreda in Holborn, central London. Etheldreda was another saint whose help was often evoked for the curing of sore throats.

> *In honour of the saint's associations, the church service includes the Blessing of the Throats, where the vicar and the local bishop hold crossed candles up to the throat of each person in attendance and say a special prayer.*

Throat blessing ceremonies take place at a number of churches in the United Kingdom and across Europe. The service at St Etheldreda's is one of the oldest, having been revived from the original Catholic rite in 1874.

The folklore year

And so the year comes round again. There are, of course, many more customs that we have not been able to include, both large and famous, or small and local, and only recognised by a few. Perhaps you will be inspired by some of the seasonal customs that we have described, to strike out into the world and seek out others yourself.

Folklore is many things, but one of the most important is that it gives us our sense of identity. These traditions and customs, once meaningful in a vital way to the members of a community, remind us of who we are, where we come from and the importance of the world around us. While many of these festivals and practices may not resonate in quite the same way as they did for our ancestors, they are an important part of our past, our present and our future. They are to be celebrated. And they are great fun, too.

If you would like to witness some of the folkloric traditions in your local area or further afield – perhaps to get a sense of the meaning and enjoyment that they hold for those taking part, and to connect you with the past – the following pages give a selection of some that you might want to try.

Seasonal Events Calendar

The following is a curated list of some of the best-known, and some of the more unusual, seasonal events which can be visited through the year.

January

Fixed dates:

1st   **Kirkwall Ba'**
Kirkwall, Orkney
A mass-participation handball game, played on the streets of Kirkwall, with teams from the upper (Uppies) and lower (Doonies) parts of town. Events begin with a procession of players, with the game commencing at 1pm. Takes place on 2nd when 1st is a Sunday.

1st   **New Year's Day Parade**
London
Street procession along a 2-mile route from the Ritz Hotel to Parliament Street, comprising marching bands, costumed entertainers, majorettes and other carnival-style elements.

6th   **Haxey Hood**
Haxey, Lincolnshire
Mass-participation game played between the residents of Haxey and Westwoodside, using a leather tube (the hood) in place of

a ball. Each team competes to score by getting the hood inside their home pub, where it stays until the following year. A traditional Fool, wearing rags, opens proceedings with a speech whilst being ritually 'smoked'. Takes place on 5th when 6th is a Sunday.

13th   **Mari Lwyd**
Upper Llangynwyd, Glamorgan
An example of the Welsh Mari Lwyd house-visiting custom, taking place at the Corner House pub. A traditional Mari Lwyd hobby horse is paraded and there is plenty of folk singing.

Variable dates:
Sherwood Twelfth Night and Fools' Parade
Saturday close to 6th | Sherwood Forest, Nottinghamshire
Costumed re-enactment of the Sheriff of Nottingham taking control of Sherwood Forest from Robin Hood and his men. Features a parade, sword fighting and a ceremony at the Major Oak.

Calverton Plough Play
Thursday to Saturday near Plough Monday (the first Monday after Epiphany on 6th) | Calverton, Nottinghamshire
Recreation of the Plough Monday folk plays historically performed by farm labourers when they returned to work. Over the three days, a number of performances based on the 'Recruiting Sergeant' mummers' play take place in local pubs.

Whittlesea Straw Bear
Weekend in the middle of the month | Whittlesey, Cambridgeshire
Revived procession of a Plough Monday straw bear – a costume
made entirely of straw, which is worn and walked through
the town. The procession comprises different styles of morris
dancing as well as a plough team pulling an old plough.

Lerwick Up Helly Aa
Last Tuesday | Lerwick, Shetland
The largest of the Up Helly Aa fire festivals, which celebrate
the Viking influences on Shetland. A procession of costumed
characters during the day is followed by the burning of a
specially constructed longship in the evening and guise dancing
(similar to mummer dancing).

February
Fixed dates:
2nd   **Candlemas Festival**
Ripon, North Yorkshire
A Christian celebration in Ripon Cathedral. Thousands of
candles are lit, symbolising Jesus as the Light of the World. Some
candles are used to form images of the building.

3rd   **Blessing the Throats**
Holborn, London
A service takes place at 1pm in St Etheldreda's Church in
celebration of the feast of St Blaise who is said to provide ease to
those suffering from throat conditions.

Variable dates:
Hackney Clowns Service
1st Sunday | Hackney, London
A church service at All Saints Church, commencing at 3pm, in celebration of the life of Joseph Grimaldi. Many of those attending are professional clowns and will be fully costumed.

Jorvik Viking Festival
Late February | York
Festival celebrating Viking culture, including historical re-enactments, guided walks and other public events. The day culminates with a battle re-enactment and fireworks.

March
Fixed dates:
1st   **St David's Day Parade**
Cardiff, Wales
A parade celebrating the patron saint of Wales is held in Cardiff city centre from approximately 12.30pm. The day is a celebration of Welsh culture with plenty of national dress and Welsh symbols present.

5th   **St Piran's Day**
Cornwall, most notably Penzance and Truro
Parades take place in several Cornish towns to celebrate the patron saint of the county. Much like St David's Day, these are a celebration of the local culture with Cornish flags, traditional food and music.

2ʒth Tichborne Dole

Tichborne, Hampshire

This is one of the oldest charity doles (a traditional offering) in Britain. Takes place at 2.30pm at Tichborne House to this day, due to a standing condition on the lease of the property. Flour is blessed by the local priest before being distributed to locals.

Variable dates:

Wife Carrying Race

Early March weekend | Dorking, Surrey

Based on Scandinavian tradition, annual 'wife' carrying (couples do not need to be married and wives do not need to be female) takes place at the Priory School from 10.30am.

Oranges and Lemons Service

3rd Thursday | London

A well-known children's rhyme begins '"Oranges and Lemons" say the bells of St Clement's. This refers to the church of St Clement Danes in The Strand, London, and is one of many churches mentioned. A service is held here each year, where local school children are presented with an orange and a lemon.

April

Fixed dates:

23rd St George's Court

Lichfield, Staffordshire

Events are held all over England in celebration of St George's Day, with many morris dancers performing. Folk plays in the mumming tradition are often performed now as well as over Christmas because of the inclusion of the characters of St George and the dragon. At the Guildhall in Lichfield a 'court' is held where the mayor appoints a number of people to traditional positions for the coming year, including two ale tasters.

30th   Beltane Fire Festival
Edinburgh
One of the largest Beltane fire celebrations, this takes place at Calton Hill. Aside from a procession and folk play performances, audiences can enjoy dancing and other street entertainment.

Variable dates:
World Dock Pudding Championship
3rd or 4th weekend | Mytholmroyd, Yorkshire
The Community Centre plays host to a competition to judge the best cooked Dock Pudding, a local food made from foraged leaves, oatmeal and onion. Dock Pudding is only made in this part of the world and the competition was designed as a way of ensuring that it did not die out.

Marsden Cuckoo Festival
Saturday late in the month | Marsden, Yorkshire
The festival culminates with a procession featuring plenty of costumes (and representations of cuckoos). The day is filled with street entertainment, craft stalls and folk play performances.

May

Fixed dates:

1st **Hobby Horse Ceremonies**

Padstow, Cornwall; Minehead, Somerset

Two of the most famous hobby horse traditions take place in the South West on this date. Both feature hoop-shaped hobby horses, accompanied by a Fool, musicians and drummers. It is likely that both of these events have origins linked to May Day fertility rites.

8th **Furry Dance**

Helston, Cornwall

A processional dance as part of Flora Day in the town. Hundreds of couples, with men wearing top hat and tails and women in ball gowns, dance their way through the streets accompanied by the town band. Folk play performances and a fair form part of the other entertainment on the day.

29th **Garland Day**

Castleton, Derbyshire

A Garland King and Queen are led on horseback through the town, accompanied by a local band. Children dance during the procession and then perform a maypole routine at the end, after which the garland is hung from the tower of the church. The event may be linked to more general Oak Apple Day traditions (see page 44).

Variable dates:

Jack in the Green

1st Saturday | Bristol

A 9-foot-tall Jack made of greenery and flowers is carried through the streets throughout the day, until at around 4pm the character ceremonially dies at Horfield Common and the foliage is distributed amongst those attending.

May Horns

1st Sunday | Penzance, Cornwall

A revival of an old Cornish custom where horns were blown to welcome the coming of the month. A party, which forms at dusk at the Tolcarne Inn in Newlyn, walks to Penzance. There are many costumed characters, a hobby horse, who ritually dies and is revived periodically along the walk, and musicians. Wear white and green and bring a whistle or other noise-making device.

June

Fixed dates:

23rd   **Midsummer Fires**

Cornwall

Known in Cornish as Tansys Golowan, a chain of beacons are lit across Cornwall on this day, with the first being the one at Carn Brea on Land's End. At each beacon, prayers are said and foliage and flowers are thrown into the flames.

29th   Warcop Rushbearing

Warcop, Cumbria

One of a few ceremonies remaining which recall the practice of renewing the rushes that used to be scattered on church floors. A procession, with children carrying crosses made of rushes, makes its way to St Columba's Church for a service at 3.15pm. Takes place on the Saturday if this date falls on a Sunday.

Variable dates:

Appleby Horse Fair

1st week | Appleby, Cumbria

A long-established Traveller fair with a focus on trading horses. Many turn up with traditionally decorated horse-drawn wagons. Horses are washed in the River Eden and exercised in the area. The fair is open to the public.

Ovingham Goose Fair

3rd Saturday | Ovingham, Northumberland

One of a number of goose fairs held across the country, most of which no longer feature geese but are a combination of fairs, market stalls and street entertainment. This one begins with a procession, generally led by someone in a goose costume.

Well Dressing

Week of 24th | Youlgrave, Derbyshire

Well dressings take place in many areas, but there are a number in Youlgrave during this week. Wells are decorated with flowers and foliage depicting either religious or local scenes.

July

Fixed dates:

4th   Baal Fire

Whalton, Northumberland

An annual bonfire, commencing at 6pm outside the Beresford Arms. Features dancing, music and morris teams. Originally a corn effigy known as a Kern Baby was burned, but now it is built outside the village hall and remains intact.

25th   Horn Fair

Ebernoe, Sussex

A traditional ram roast, taking place on the cricket field in celebration of St James's Day. The roasting ram is carried in a procession in the early afternoon and is served at the end of a cricket match that takes place all day, along with a fair and other entertainment. A song for the Horn Fair is also sung.

Variable dates:

Winchester Hat Fair

1st weekend | Winchester, Hampshire

A festival of street theatre which has been running for over 50 years. The event, which is free to attend, takes its name from the fact that donations were traditionally placed into a hat.

Rose Petal Sunday

Sunday close to 7th | Salisbury, Wiltshire

A service takes place at St Thomas's Church in remembrance of the remains of St Thomas Becket being moved to Canterbury

Cathedral in 1220. After the service, sacks of rose petals are emptied from the top of the church tower.

World Peashooting Championships
2nd Saturday | Witcham, Cambridgeshire
One of any number of curious alternative seasonal sporting events which take place across Britain. The Peashooting Championships are held on the village green. Those taking part stand 12 feet from a 1-foot-wide target and are allowed five shots in each round.

August
Fixed dates:
5th   **Brigg Fair**
Brigg, Lincolnshire
An ancient horse fair organised by the Travelling community, originating from a charter granted in 1205. Horses are ridden through the town streets, with many pulling traditional caravans and vardos (a Romani wagon). A folk song was written about the fair. Takes place on 4th if 5th is a Sunday.

24th   **Bartlemas Bun Run**
Sandwich, Kent
A service in the chapel at the Hospital of St Bartholomew is followed by a race around the perimeter of the building for children, said to be symbolic of past pilgrimages. After the race, children are presented with a currant bun. Adults receive

a traditional hard biscuit which is stamped with the Sandwich coat of arms.

Variable dates:

Egton Bridge Gooseberry Show

1st Tuesday | Egton Bridge, North Yorkshire

The longest established gooseberry show in Britain, with the heaviest berries sometimes exceeding 60 grammes. The Gooseberry Society is responsible for the weighing process, using traditional apothecary scales. Fruit is assessed in the morning and put out for viewing in the afternoon.

Burry Man

2nd Friday | Queensferry, Lothian

A custom which is believed to have originated as a form of bringing luck. The Burry Man is a man who wears a costume covered in thousands of burdock heads. He spends most of the day parading through the town, accompanied by two attendants wearing suits.

Waiters' Races

Late August Friday | Dartmouth, Devon

Competitors (who must be genuinely employed as waiters) race the length of the street carrying a tray and glass. Halfway through the race they must fill the glass with beer, with the winner being the one with the fullest glass at the end of the race. The event is part of the Dartmouth Royal Regatta weekend.

September

3rd   Battle of Worcester Commemoration
Worcester, Guildhall and Fort Royal Hill
Organised by the Battle of Worcester Society, the
commemoration begins with a parade from the Guildhall at
6pm, which features Civil War re-enactors. A service is held at
Fort Royal Hill after the parade.

Variable dates:

Clipping the Church
Sunday close to 8th | Wirksworth, Derbyshire
One of several survivors of an old ceremony where the
congregation joins hands in a circle around the outside of the
church building. The 'clipping' here takes place as part of the
Sunday service, with a procession being led out of the church
through the west door to make the circle.

Abbots Bromley Horn Dance
*Monday after the Sunday following 4th | Abbots Bromley,
Staffordshire*
Probably one of the oldest and most well-known seasonal
events in the country, the Horn Dance is performed by six
men carrying antlers, accompanied by a hobby horse and other
characters and musicians. Church services take place at the
beginning and end of the day.

Widecombe Fair

Second Tuesday | Widecombe-in-the-Moor, Devon

A traditional country fair which has become famous, particularly because of the folk song telling of Uncle Tom Cobley and his associates borrowing a grey mare from Tom Pearce to ride to Widecombe. You can expect to see the characters from the song during the day, both as costumed locals and also in the gift shops.

October

Fixed dates:

2nd   **Old Man's Day**

Braughing, Hertfordshire

A custom which remembers Matthew Wall, a resident of the town in the 16th century who would have been buried alive had his coffin not been dropped on the way to the funeral, bringing him out of his unconscious state. The vicar recounts the story, the church bells are rung and local children ceremonially sweep the route along which the coffin would have been carried.

31st   **Samhuinn Parade**

Edinburgh, Scotland

Fire festival for Samhain, or Hallowe'en, organised by the Beltane Fire Society. Musicians, dancers and costumed characters provide a dramatic rendition of the end of the summer season and the start of darker times.

Variable dates:

The Big Apple

2nd full weekend | Much Marcle, Herefordshire

A celebration of the apple harvest in the area. Events include tastings, apple identification experts and demonstrations of traditional cider making.

Harvest Festival Corn Dolly Display

2nd weekend | Siddington, Cheshire

All Saints Church displays hundreds of corn dollies alongside seasonal fruits and vegetables. The dollies were all made by local historian and collector Raymond Rush.

Wild Hunt

Late Saturday | Glastonbury, Somerset

Morris dancing displays are followed by a big procession through the streets that marks the end of summer. Two dragons – one red and one white – are a main feature, along with musicians and drums and other costumed performers. There is a ritualistic battle between the two dragons. The white dragon is victorious, showing that winter has overcome summer.

November

Fixed dates:

5th   **Flaming Tar Barrels**

Ottery St Mary, Devon

Wooden barrels coated in tar and set on fire are run through the streets of the town, carried on the shoulders of the men and women who take part. Many thousands attend the event and a sense of self-preservation is vital! Takes place on Saturday 4th if 5th is a Sunday.

5th   **Turning the Devil's Stone**
Shebbear, Devon
Every year on this date, at 8pm, local residents use crowbars to turn over a large boulder that sits on the green outside The Devil's Stone Inn, whilst the local bell-ringers sound a badly tuned peal on the church bells. There are many versions of the story behind the stone, but it is generally accepted that the village will have bad luck for the year if the stone is not turned.

Variable dates:
Antrobus Soulcakers
First half of the month | Antrobus, Cheshire
Performances of a traditional hero-and-combat mummers' play take place in various pubs in the area both on All Souls' Eve and on the two weekends after that date.

Carnival and Tar Barrels
2nd Saturday | Hatherleigh, Devon
A torchlit procession, local brass bands and majorettes head up a large carnival consisting of themed floats and costumed walkers. After the carnival has taken place, a number of tar barrels are set alight and pulled down the street on a sled. If you are up early enough, a similar thing is done with barrels at 5am.

St Clement's Day
Saturday close to 23rd | Okehampton, Devon
St Clement's Day blacksmithing events take place at Finch
Foundry, the National Trust's water-powered forge. Master
blacksmiths demonstrate their skills and the tradition of 'firing
the anvil', where gunpowder is lit to test the anvil's integrity.
Takes place throughout the day.

December

Fixed dates:

21st   **Montol Festival**

Penzance, Cornwall

A more recently created tradition which is rooted very firmly
in Cornish culture and customs, with much to see. The Montol
procession takes place at 6pm and includes musicians, costumed
characters, a hobby horse, dancers and mummers, overseen by
the Lord of Misrule. You can also witness the old custom of
Chalking the Mock, where a stick figure is drawn in chalk onto a
yule log (the Mock) before it is placed on a fire.

24th   **Poor Old Hoss**

Richmond, North Yorkshire

Around lunchtime at the market in Richmond, a mumming
group dressed in traditional hunting garb lead out a hobby horse
built in the Mari Lwyd style, with a horse skull on a pole. A
special song is sung and the 'hoss' ritually dies and is revived by
the sound of a hunting horn.

26th   Knaresborough Tug of War
Knaresborough, North Yorkshire
A traditional Boxing Day tug of war competition which has
been held for decades at Low Bridge, spanning the River Nidd.
Teams from the two pubs on either side of the river compete,
using an exceptionally long rope which crosses the entire river.

Variable dates:
Whitby Krampus Run
1st Saturday | Whitby, North Yorkshire
Started in 2015, the Krampus Run at Whitby was the first
organised incursion of this creature from the lore of the
Alpine areas of Europe into Britain. In line with the idea of the
Krampus punishing naughty children, costumed characters may
give candy canes to those young people they consider to be good.

Holy Thorn Cutting
Around 13th | Glastonbury, Somerset
A flowering thorn at Glastonbury is said, as far as legend tells,
to have grown from the staff carried by Joseph of Arimathea
when he visited the area. The current tree is believed to have
been grown from cuttings taken from the original thorn which
was pulled up in Puritanical times. Each year a cutting is taken
by the mayor and a child from a local school, and are sent to the
reigning monarch to place on the Christmas Day dining table.

Index